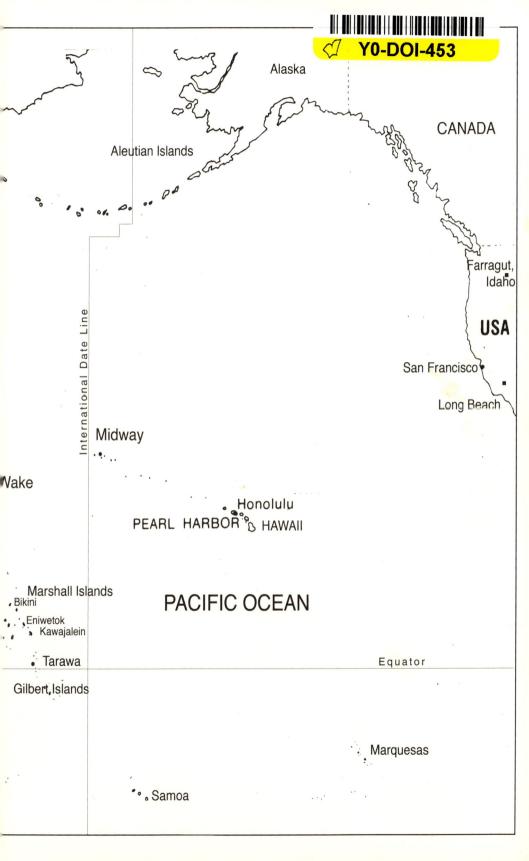

TWENTY-TWO MONTHS

THE UNTOLD STORY
OF A YOUNG SAILOR IN THE
PACIFIC THEATER OF OPERATIONS
DURING WWII

JAMES REDING

PARK PLACE PUBLICATIONS
PACIFIC GROVE, CALIFORNIA

Copyright © 2005 by James Reding

Published and printed in the United States of America

FIRST EDITION

ISBN 1-877809-48-9

Library of Congress Control Number: 2005924794

PUBLISHED BY
Park Place Publications
P.O. Box 829
Pacific Grove, CA 93950
www.parkplacepublications.com

DEDICATION

I would like to offer a special recognition
to my wife Barbara to whom I dedicate this book. Without her
patience, encouragement and guidance, I would be back at page
one. Also, would like to thank my family, former shipmates,
neighbors and friends for their interest and assistance.

CONTENTS

GLOSSARY
ABBREVIATIONS, ORGANIZATIONS, AND TERMS

APA   Amphibious Personnel Attack troopship

aft   Toward the stern or rear of a ship

Allies   A group of nations joined together for mutual assistance. A term used during World War II for England, France, United States and the other countries that joined them in their conflict against the Axis nations

Axis   An alliance of nations. During World War II Germany, Italy and Japan were the primary Axis nation

blimp   A lighter-than-air ship that was 251 feet long, 62 feet wide and 17 feet high. They had a range of over 2,000 miles at a speed of 40 knots. They carried a crew of three officers and six men. Their primary use was for coastal anti-submarine and mine patrols

boatswain's pipe   Whistle used by boatswain's mates to relay information to the crew

Captain's Gig   A boat, which at times would be used exclusively for the captain of the ship

CIC   Combat Information Center aboard a US naval vessel. The nerve center of the ship where battle information is collected and evaluated

Condition 1 Able   Duty stations during the process of debarking troops.

D-Day.   Debarkation Day during a combat landing. (Every combat landing has a D-Day)

dirigible   A 785-foot long lighter than air ship with a crew of twelve and capable of carrying one ton of bombs. Their range was over 2,000 miles

Draft   To be conscripted into the military; a group of military personnel being transferred from one station to another; the depth of the hull of a vessel under the water's surface portion of a ship

Frogmen   A nickname for members of the U.S. Navy's Underwater Demolition Teams

fore   Front or forward portion of a ship

General Quarters (GQ)   Battle stations aboard ship

Higgins boats   Landing craft designed and manufactured by Andrew Jackson Higgins (1886–1952). Mr. Higgins' New Orleans-based company was the major producer of those wooden hulled (LCVP) boats

Leathernecks   A nickname for the United States Marines

LCVP (Landing Craft Vehicles Personnel) (VP Boat)   A shallow draft 36 foot landing craft capable of carrying troops and/or small vehicles through the surf onto a beach

LCP (Landing Craft Personnel)   A shallow draft 36-foot landing craft used to carry troops through the surf onto a beach

leave   Permission to leave a ship or a base for a period of days

lee   Downwind, an area sheltered from the wind

liberty   Permission to leave a ship or base for a period of hours

Liberty boat   A small craft used to carry personnel from their ships to shore for their liberty

Liberty ship   A type of merchant ship constructed during World War II

Minesweepers   Wooden hulled 97 to 135 foot ships designed to "sweep" or clear coastal mine fields; some of the larger 185 footers had steel hulls

NCOIC   Non-Commissioned Officer-In-Charge

OIC   Officer-In-Charge

Paravane   Small airplane-shaped water-kite device attached to a steel cable and trolled from the bow of the ship to locate submerged mines.

Port   Left side of a ship; also a place to dock or anchor a ship

POW   Prisoner-of-war

Seabees   The Navy's construction battalion, as the Corps of Engineers would be to the Army

Shore Patrol (SP's)   The Navy's police force, "the cop on the beat"

starboard   Right side of a ship

UDT   Underwater Demolition Team. The Navy's "Frogmen." Their job was to clear obstructions on hostile beaches

windward   Toward the direction the wind is blowing

TWENTY-TWO MONTHS

THE UNTOLD STORY
OF A YOUNG SAILOR IN THE
PACIFIC THEATER OF OPERATIONS
DURING WWII

BACKGROUND

AMERICA UNDER ATTACK

On Sunday morning, December 7, 1941, I was in the ninth grade at Woodrow Wilson Junior High School in San Jose. That morning, I was going to take a ride with two friends from Bellarmine College Preparatory whom I'd known since grammar school. When we were seated in the car, the driver started the engine and turned on the radio.

The radio announcer, with unusual excitement in his voice, was reporting a news bulletin. He said that Japanese airplanes had attacked our ships at a Naval base, called Pearl Harbor, in the Pacific Ocean. The base was located on an island, which he pronounced as "OO Ahh You." We didn't know where "OO Ahh You" (Oahu) or Pearl Harbor were located. We had never heard of them. We were soon to find out.

That Sunday morning the direction of our lives changed. Each one of us was destined to become directly involved in the most devastating conflict in the known history of mankind.

Without warning, Japanese aircraft attacked our fleet at the United States Naval Base at Pearl Harbor, and the United States Army and Air Corps facilities in the Hawaiian Islands. The bombing and strafing of our military bases changed America and the world, as we knew it.

I got out of the car and went into the house. My parents were listening to the news report on the radio. They were stunned. No one seemed to fully realize what was happening. We knew it wasn't good, but no one was able to grasp the impact of the moment. On December 7, 1941, which would later be called Pearl Harbor Day, we were so naively unprepared.

SAN JOSE GOES TO WAR

That afternoon and evening, my family gathered around the radio listening to the latest updates of the attack. There were reports that our bases in the Philippines and two other islands in the mid-Pacific—Wake and Guam—were also being attacked by the Japanese.

The information we received was erratic; yet in this atmosphere of uncertainty, in our community, a calm confusion seemed to prevail.

The next day, Monday, December 8, 1941, President Franklin Roosevelt called for a joint session of Congress. We intently listened on the radio to the President's distinctive voice as he gave his powerful "Day of Infamy Speech." With historical eloquence, he asked Congress for a declaration of war against the Empire of Japan.

Confused as to what we should do, we went about our everyday activities with the constant reminder about what had happened. Overnight, San Jose began to change. The first telltale signs were on the highways around our community.

San Jose is located along the Old Spanish Mission Trail, better known as the El Camino Real, the King's Highway. This was the historic route between the San Francisco area in Northern California and Los Angeles-San Diego in Southern California.

Automobiles and trucks traveling south from the Bay Area rail and shipping hubs passed directly through San Jose. The main route of the two-lane highway was only a block away from our house. From our front porch, we could watch the highway traffic as it passed through town.

A few hours after we first heard about the attack on our ships at Pearl Harbor, convoys of Army trucks and armored vehicles began rolling down our city streets heading north.

Standing with my folks on the corner of Second and Reed Streets, I watched two dozen trucks, a small tank carried on a flatbed trailer and some armored cars—their machine guns manned by somber-looking soldiers wearing the WWI Doughboy-style helmets—drive past us.

We didn't know where the military came from or where they were going. My parents thought they might be from Army bases near the city of Monterey, south of San Jose.

For the next few days, an almost continual flow of convoys moved through town. The major traffic was northbound. Our guess was that the soldiers and their equipment were being sent to reinforce the garrisons at the forts in San Francisco or for possible transportation overseas.

After the initial shock from the attack, we finally began to realize that we were "at war." Military personnel were assigned and stationed within the city limits of San Jose. Almost overnight, our sleepy little agricultural town, which was popularly known for its location in the "Valley of the Heart's Delight," was turned into an armed camp. During the Christmas vacation many of the soldiers were temporarily housed in our schools and public buildings.

Sandbags and 30-mm machine gun nests were placed on the taller downtown buildings such as the Sainte Claire Hotel at Market and San Carlos Street, and the Bank of America Building at First and Santa Clara Streets. The transformation was amazing.

"OVER THERE, AND OVER HERE"

Prior to December 7th, the Atlantic and Pacific Oceans were considered to be comfort-zone barriers from the brutality of foreign wars. We believed that we were oceans away from the conflicts in the other parts of the world. We felt protected from the hostilities.

Even after the Japanese bombed Pearl Harbor and Congress declared war, the average American pretty much went about his or her daily activities. The prevailing attitude seemed to be that the conflict was "Over There." This feeling was similar to America's participation in the "Great War" which later would be known as World War I.

Cities along the coastline—especially on our more heavily populated Atlantic Seaboard—conducted business as usual. During the first few months in 1942, many of the coastal cities naively continued to light up their communities at night as if nothing had happened.

These communities didn't realize that groups of German submarines were operating in the Atlantic waters seaward of the shipping lanes. These Nazi U-boat "wolf packs" were stalking their unsuspecting prey.

As our freighters traveled the eastern coastal sea-lanes from Maine to Florida, the nighttime lights from seaside cities outlined the vessels. The silhouetted ships became perfect targets for the aggressive Nazi submarine captains. The German commanders had a shooter's holiday.

Almost at will, their torpedoes sank our merchant ships.

In the spring of 1942, the tentacles of Japanese aggression reached deep into Southeast Asia and the Western Pacific. Military forces of the Japanese Empire inflicted devastating losses on American, Philippine, Australian, British, French, Dutch and Chinese civilians and military personnel.

Emperor Hirohito's armies and naval forces quickly captured the Philippines, Wake Island and Guam along with other key American and British possessions in the Central and Western Pacific Ocean.

The Empire of the Rising Sun was on the offense in China and the Malaysian peninsula. Soon the strategically key cities of Manila and Singapore fell. Australia was vulnerable to an invasion. The Japanese military seemed almost unstoppable.

Americans were painfully jolted into the realization that we were in a conflict for the survival of our nation. The war was "Over Here" as well as "Over There." Our country developed a firmness that we were not going to concede to the brutally aggressive Nazi and Japanese war machines. As a nation, we bonded together to face the challenges of the unknown.

Survival strategies used by besieged cities and towns in England were modified and enacted. Stringent wartime regulations were established and enforced, especially along the coasts and in the larger cities. Nighttime blackout procedures were rigidly followed in all sensitive areas.

America's West Coast (Alaska, Washington, Oregon and California)—due to its proximity to Asia—feared Japan as the major aggressor. An attempted invasion by Japanese forces along our Western Seaboard was considered a real possibility. Therefore, civilian activities were dramatically curtailed along the Pacific coastline from Canada to Mexico.

Many of California's luxury hotels along the coast were acquired by the military and used for the duration of the War. The prestigious Del Monte Resort Hotel in Monterey became a training school for officers, and the popular Casa Del Rey Hotel in Santa Cruz became a Rest and Rehabilitation (R&R) center for the wounded and those suffering from battle fatigue.

In December 1941, soon after war was declared, large, steel-mesh anti-submarine nets were positioned in the water across the entrances to our major shipping ports and anchorages. The net that helped to protect San Francisco Bay was placed across the seaward mouth of the Golden Gate passageway to the harbor.

At dawn the net was drawn open. At dusk it was protectively located across the opening, thereby closing the entrance to all shipping. Enemy submarines or naval vessels were not going to be given any easy targets of opportunity in our waterways.

We had learned that our homeland was vulnerable. Early in the months of 1942, Japanese submarines were spotted off the shores of California. An enemy submarine fired twenty-six shells into an oil refinery storage facility at Goleta, a small coastal community near Santa Barbara, California. This was reportedly the first direct attack by a foreign nation on the mainland soil of the United States since the War of 1812, which was 130 years earlier.

The extended coastlines of the United States had numerous, isolated areas that were ideal locations for the enemy to land saboteurs and guerrilla-warfare personnel.

Reports were circulated that Germans saboteurs had landed from submarines onto some of our sparsely settled Atlantic Seaboard beaches. Also, it was reported that the Japanese were attempting to or had landed hostile forces along the coast of California.

DEFENDING OUR SHORES

Total war measures were enacted. Troops were stationed at strategic seaside locations and multiple layers of protective barbed wire were strung along any potential hostile landing sites. In Northern California, the shores of Monterey Bay bristled with newly established Army infantry, air corps and field artillery camps. These hastily constructed military facilities were also protectively enclosed by barbed wire. Cannons were positioned so that their shells could destroy any enemy forces that tried to approach our beaches.

Strict military control was imposed. Most seaside areas were declared "off limits." Curfews were established from dusk to dawn. Blackout rules were imposed and rigidly enforced. Civilians considered to be a threat to the war effort were relocated to inland communities and camps.

Nighttime was considered the period of greatest danger from enemy attack or infiltration. On foot, horseback and in motorized vehicles, military personnel, armed with weapons containing live ammunition patrolled vulnerable beaches bluffs and roads.

Local civilians volunteered to be air raid wardens and coastal watchers. Many of them were Veterans of World War I and were too old for military service. Diligently, with military bearing, these citizen wardens manned their posts along our West Coast seven days per week, twenty-four hours per day in rotating two- to four-hour shifts.

Their assignment was to ensure that unauthorized persons did not enter restricted areas, and that the nighttime blackout rules and curfews were enforced. A similar program was enacted along the Eastern and Southern Seaboards of our country. Almost every American from eight to eighty became involved in the war effort.

After sundown, driving along the shoreline roads was restricted. Vehicles that were authorized to travel in the area at night had to have specially designed metal covers over their headlights. These shields permitted a small, rectangular beam of light to shine through a slit in the cover allowing only minimal visibility of the roadway ahead.

Also in the coastal zone, residential and business windows were required to be covered with material that emitted no light. Most people used what they called blackout-curtains. After sunset, those special curtains were to be drawn across all windows.

At nighttime, due to the stringent wartime-restrictions, most of the people residing in seaside communities stayed at home or within walking distance from their house.

Some of the more popular home entertainment activities were visiting neighbors, playing cards, putting jigsaw puzzles together, reading and listening to the radio. Among the favorite radio entertainers were Jack Benny, Fibber Magee and Molly, Amos and Andy, Fred Allen and the beloved Kate Smith whose powerful rendition of the song "God Bless America" was a national favorite.

RATIONING IN AMERICA

In April 1942, rationing was imposed on food, clothing, gasoline, tires and any other items vital to the war effort. The governmental agency that was responsible for the rationing program was the Office of Price

Administration (OPA).

To have an equitable system for the allocation of food and other scarce items, the OPA issued booklets of ration stamps. For food, the stamps were red, green, brown or blue. Each rationed item was categorized, and allocated a point valuation depending upon its size, quantity and scarcity.

The stamps were issued according to the number of people in each household. One member of each family or household could register for the entire family. My parents had coupon booklets with ration stamps for the five of us (my mother, father, brother, sister and me).

In order to purchase meat, butter and other everyday items required the dollars or cents price of the product plus food stamps. The color of the stamp and its point value determined what a customer was allowed to buy. Hamburger might be twenty-five cents and "five points" per pound. People could earn extra points by participating in recycling programs.

Also, families could supplement their food supplies by growing vegetables in their yards, or in empty lots in what were known as "Victory Gardens." It was a time when the entire nation mobilized. Americans saved string, tin foil, scrap metal and anything else that could be of benefit to the war effort.

From May to December 1942, gasoline rationing was phased into the conservation program. Each automobile or truck with a valid registration and current state license plate was eligible for a rationing sticker, which would be affixed to the windshield.

The stickers were designated A, B, or C, depending on the occupation of the owner in relation to their contribution to the country's needs. "C" stickers were usually issued to doctors and law-enforcement personnel.

Also, there were separate stickers for VIPs, such as local politicians, that let them have an increased quantity of rationed automotive items. There was such a public outcry of indignation over this privileged treatment for the so-called "public servants" that this special category was eventually blended into the general public's sticker program.

The family car—considered a "non-essential vehicle"—received an "A" sticker, which meant that the owner would be allocated, and allowed to purchase, only four gallons of gasoline a week. Most cars had "A" stickers. If you didn't use public transportation, you either walked or rode a bicycle.

SELECTIVE SERVICE SYSTEM (THE DRAFT)

Recruitment and drafting for the armed forces was accelerated. The personnel build-up of our military services went from a few hundred thousand in 1940, to over twelve million on active duty when the war ended in 1945.

Congress enacted the Selective Training and Service Act (Draft) in September 1940. Young men, ages twenty-one to thirty, were eligible to be drafted into the military on an "as needed" basis. At first draftees were assigned to the Army. After the war began, the compulsory age for service was modified to be from eighteen to forty-five. The conscription was expanded to include the Army, Navy and the Marines. With their parent's consent, seventeen-year-olds could voluntarily enlist in the U.S. Navy or the Marine Corps.

There were four basic draft classifications. 1A: eligible for immediate induction into the armed forces; 2A: a draft-age male working in a defense-related industry such a shipyard, aircraft factory or food-production; 3A: married with children; and 4F: physically or mentally unfit for military service.

There was also a special classification for those with religious or personal convictions who were opposed to aggressive solutions to the problems between the nations of the world. This group was classified as conscientious objectors (COs). Even though a young man might be classified as a CO, it didn't necessarily mean that he would not go into the armed forces. Some COs went into military service as medics and served their country with pride and honor. Lew Ayres, a Hollywood movie star, was a CO. As a medic in the U.S. Army, he contributed to the war effort with distinction.

Almost every able-bodied male eighteen to forty-five years of age either volunteered, or was drafted into the military. Many married men—even though they were exempt from military service —volunteered to do their duty. A young man of military age who was not in uniform was often viewed with suspicion. The spirit of patriotism was reflected throughout the country. Almost everyone—in one way or another—helped with the war effort.

WOMEN OF AMERICA STEP FORWARD

The 19th or Suffrage Amendment to the United States Constitution had been passed in 1920, which was only twenty-one years before Pearl Harbor was attacked. This amendment granted women in the United States the right to vote. In 1941, even though women had the right to vote, the opportunities available to them were still restricted by tradition and attitude.

At that time, upon graduation from high school, most young women in Northern California joined the work force for a few years until they were married. In San Jose, the primary jobs available to them were as telephone operators, sales clerks, secretaries, waitresses or cannery workers.

With the onset of the war, when the men entered the armed forces, the women of America stepped forward and successfully filled almost every workforce-position and profession, which traditionally were held by males. The country-and the world-were soon to learn that American women through their outstanding effort and performance in the home-front workforce far exceeded any limited traditional expectations. Also, with competence and distinction, they held almost every non-combatant position in our military forces. Many of them volunteered to go into the following newly established branches of the Armed Forces. These were:

Navy: WAVES (Women Accepted for Volunteer Emergency Service)
Army: WAACs (Women Army Auxiliary Corps)
Marines: Marine Corps Women's Reserve (better known as
           Women Marines or Marines)
Coast Guard: SPARs —Coast Guard Women's Reserve
Army Air Corp: WASPs (Women Auxiliary Service Pilots)

Women from eighteen-to-sixty worked in the munitions factories, shipyards and manufacturing plants throughout the country. They were mechanics, riveters, welders, heavy-equipment and crane operators. Affectionately, some were known as "Rosie the Riveter."

In addition to working ten to twelve hour shifts in the defense industry, the women of America were also the foundation and stability for the families on the home front, and the emotional support for loved-ones serving in war zones throughout the world.

AMERICA MOBILIZES

In key strategic locations throughout the country, there was a burgeoning of defense factories, plants and shipyards. Production of vitally needed items received top priority. Financial rewards were given to industrial leaders as incentives for them to meet the logistical challenges for a global war. Cost was a secondary consideration. Many government contracts for essential items were based on the cost plus an additional percentage of the cost as profit.

The Santa Clara Valley food industry was considered vital to the defense of our country. Canneries and food processing plants were geared for maximum production. To meet these sudden workforce demands, housewives, high school students and the elderly filled many of the defense-based jobs. During the summers, elementary school children picked fruit in the orchards. High school students worked in the canneries and in other jobs as part of the war effort. Major lifestyle adjustments were made as the nation evolved into a wartime footing. America mobilized for its survival. In this atmosphere, the military came first and the needs of the civilians came second.

In the San Francisco Bay Area, military bases and wartime industries—especially shipyards—sprang up at almost every buildable location. A contractor named Henry Kaiser—who helped to build the Hoover Dam near Las Vegas, Nevada—was one of the organizational geniuses behind the assembly line shipbuilding program. Under Henry Kaiser's leadership, mud flats around the perimeter of the San Francisco Bay were dredged, drained and excavated to provide sites for large shipbuilding complexes.

Merchant ships were constructed at shipyards located at Richmond, on the Oakland side of the Bay, in San Francisco at Hunter's Point and in the city of South San Francisco, just north of the present San Francisco International Airport. In Marin County, there was a shipyard and the Hamilton Field Army Air Corps base. On the other side of the bay near Vallejo, Mare Island had a large naval ship-repair-yard and a submarine base.

The shipyards ran twenty-four hours a day, seven days per week. Workers were divided into two twelve-hour or three eight-hour shifts. They prided themselves in being able to construct a ship, from laying the keel to launching, in less than thirty days.

Treasure Island, the site of the 1939 World's Fair, was converted to a naval base. The Alameda Naval Air Station became a major facility for U.S. Navy aircraft carriers. East of Oakland, near Livermore, the Navy constructed an inland naval base called Camp Shoemaker. Later, it was re-named Camp Parks.

Military hospitals were established or expanded throughout the San Francisco Bay Area. Major naval medical facilities were located on Mare Island and in the hills of Oakland (Oak Knoll Naval Hospital). The Army had Letterman Hospital at the Presidio in San Francisco.

With its large natural harbor, docks, railroad yards and warehouses, the San Francisco Bay area rapidly developed into a major logistical wartime center. Troops and materials were shipped to the far reaches of the Pacific and Indian Oceans. Wounded and rotating personnel returning to the States through the Golden Gate received medical treatment at one of the military hospitals, or were reassigned to other units.

Santa Clara Valley was sprinkled with military bases. The largest was Moffett Field Naval Air Station located a few miles north of San Jose. The Navy established the base in 1933 for its expanding fleet of the huge football-shaped air-ships known as dirigibles. They were the largest of this class. The smaller versions are called blimps. The Air Station was named Moffett Field in memory of the Navy's Chief of the Bureau of Aeronautics, Rear Admiral William A. Moffett, who was killed in the crash of the dirigible USS Akron.

To protect those enormous aircrafts from the elements, "Hangar Number One" was constructed. It is a huge curved shaped 198-foot tall structure with a footprint that covers over eight acres. Hangar Number One's first occupant was the dirigible USS Macon. On February 12, 1935, with the reported loss of two lives, the Macon crashed in a storm off the rugged coast of Big Sur, California.

Through the subsequent years, smaller dirigibles (blimps) were con-structed. They were primarily designed for use as aerial anti-submarine and mine-patrols. During World War II, Moffett Field became a major facility for our blimps. In 1943, two additional hangars were constructed on the base to house those smaller lighter-than- air-ships.

When the war was over, that type of air-ship was phased-out of the Navy's inventory. Today, motorist traveling along Highway 101, near Sunnyvale, California, can easily see those three huge landmark hangars.

CHAPTER I

THE WAR TOUCHES OUR FAMILY

In 1942, America's wartime casualty losses throughout the world were so great that a "curtain of silence" prevailed. It was very difficult—if not impossible—to obtain any official information about what had happened to loved-ones reported, "missing in action." Through censorship the extent of our losses was suppressed.

In the fall of 1942, my mother received word that her forty-four-year-old brother, Charles L. Fitzgerald, was missing in action in the South Atlantic Ocean. Charlie was a little over two years older than Mom. Since childhood, they were very close. The news deeply saddened her.

When my mother was engaged to my father, Charlie took her to Gumps, an exclusive department store in San Francisco and told her to select any china that she wanted. It would be his wedding present to her. To the day that Mom died, just two months before of her ninetieth birthday, that china was one of her most treasured possessions.

Charlie had been in the merchant marine as a chief engineer in the 1930's, but left the sea when he married and had a family. When the war broke out, he was working in San Francisco as a boilermaker.

Thrust into a worldwide conflict...President Roosevelt called upon our experienced seamen of all ages to become crews for the merchant ships under construction in the shipyards of America. The freighters were needed to carry supplies to and from the four corners of the world.

At that time Uncle Charlie was deferred from military service. He was in the 3A category for the draft because he had a wife and two children plus he was almost forty-five years old. But Charlie had the experience needed to help man the ships of our rapidly expanding fleet of merchant ships. Deciding to help the war effort by going back to sea, he signed on as the first engineer aboard the Liberty ship, SS *Stephen Hopkins*. The newly constructed freighter was launched in May of 1942, from the Richmond, California shipyard. This would be its first and last voyage.

For over six months all we knew was that Charlie was "Missing In Action." The curtain of silence had fallen over his ship and its crew. We did not have any idea what happened to him or his ship until early 1943. One of his shipmates from the *Hopkins* unexpectedly called my mother and asked if he could stop by our house. During his visit, we learned what happened to Charlie and their ship.

On September 27th, the SS *Stephen Hopkins*, under the command of Captain Paul Buck, was in the Atlantic off the coast of South America. The freighter was traveling from Cape Town, South Africa to Paramaribo in Dutch Guiana with a crew of 40 merchant sailors, 15 US Navy armed-guard-gunners and one passenger.

The *Hopkins* had a 37-mm gun on the bow, several anti-aircraft guns on the superstructure and on the fantail was a 4-inch cannon. The Navy had provided the armed guard to man the guns.

The weapons on the slow-moving freighters were more of a confidence factor for the crew than any significant threat to attacking enemy ships, submarines, or airplanes.

In those same waters were two Nazi warships, the *Stier* and the *Tannenfels*. They were part of a group of German raiders that were disguised as merchantmen. With wooden sideboards hiding their cannons and flying the flag of a neutral nation, they sailed the sea-lanes of the Atlantic and Indian Oceans looking for unsuspecting prey. Their goal was to intercept and if possible capture the merchantmen and seize their cargo.

Once a lightly armed allied freighter was spotted; the warships would drop their sideboards, thereby revealing their guns, lower the neutral flag; raise the ensign of the German navy and shoot a warning-shot across the victim's bow. If the ship did not stop and surrender, the raiders would open-fire to damage and if necessary sink the vessel.

Around 9 a.m. on the morning of September 27, 1942, the raiders *Stier* and *Tannenfels* sighted the *Hopkins*. Following the standard intercept procedure, the Nazi warships dropped their wooden sideboards, ran up the ensigns of the German Navy and fired a warning "heave to" shot across the Liberty ship's bow.

Upon seeing the enemy with their far superior firepower, most merchantmen would have surrendered. Captain Buck decided to fight. He gave the orders to sound General Quarters for "All Hands To Man Your Battle Stations."

My Uncle Charlie had just completed his watch and was sitting on his bunk when the general alarm sounded. He quickly started moving towards his combat duty station.

Seeing that the crew of the merchant ship was preparing to do battle, the Nazi gunners fired a salvo of shells, which struck the freighter amid-ship killing Charlie.

After receiving continuous subsequent barrages of shelling from the German ships, the Hopkins was afire and almost dead in the water. Despite the overwhelming odds against them, the courageous US Navy's Armed Guard gunners with the assistance of members of the merchant crew fought back. In the face of mounting causalities those remarkable sailors tenaciously fired their 37-mm bow gun and their 4-inch canon on the fantail until they ran out of ammunition.

Ablaze and listing, Captain Buck reluctantly gave the order to abandon ship. While still under heavy shellfire from the Germans, the surviving members of the crew managed to launch and get into the undamaged life rafts and lifeboats. As they were rowing away from the fiery hulk of their ship, to their amazement they saw that the *Stier* was also ablaze and sinking.

The gunners from the *Hopkins* with their smaller, shorter-ranged weapons had inflicted sufficient damage to mortally wound one of the attacking enemy warships. They also damaged the Raider *Tannenfels* so severely that it was put out of action and had to limp to the nearest port for repairs.

Of the 56 people aboard the *Hopkins*, only 8 members of the crew, 6 armed-guardsmen and the passenger survived the battle and the harrowing ordeal of drifting on the open sea for several weeks before they reached the coast of South America. Captain Paul Buck, the commanding officer, was last seen swimming towards a life raft.

The conflict between the lightly armed freighter and the two German raider warships added a remarkable chapter to the annals of the history of America's merchant fleet. Through an Executive Order issued by President Harry Truman, in August 1946, the SS *Stephen Hopkins* received the honor and distinction of being designated a "Gallant Ship" of the United States Maritime Service for "the stark courage of her crew in their heroic stand against overpowering odds..." Today, along the water-front in San Francisco, a sister ship, the SS *Jeremiah O'Brien*, has been preserved and is open for the public to visit.

My Uncle Charlie's death affected our entire family. Personally, I wanted to go into the military as soon as I could.

At San Jose High School, the school I was attending, we had an Army State Guard Cadet Program. The State Guard Cadets could provide additional forces for the defense of our coastline if the enemy invaded us.. After hearing that Charlie was "Missing In Action," I joined the Cadet Program. At that time I was fifteen-years-old.

As a cadet, we received credit for a Physical Education class. Our instructor in charge, or "commandant," was Sam Della Maggiore, our wrestling coach and Physical Education teacher.

We wore Army khaki summer uniforms. Our rifles were wooden stage props. Our drill instructor was Harley "Rock" Adams. He was about twenty-years-old and had been in the U.S. Marine Corps. They said he had a medical discharge from the Corps. Rock Adams taught us the rudiments of rifle drills and formation marching. He trained us to be future Marines.

If our coastline were invaded, our high-school-cadet crop of fifteen-to-eighteen-year-olds would be assigned real rifles and would be deployed where needed in the defense of our shorelines.

In December 1943, I was sixteen-years-old. During Christmas vacation from school, I went to the Santa Cruz Beach and boardwalk with some of my classmates. We were surprised to see some Marines slowly walking along the beach. A few of them were in their hospital clothes, but most of them were informally dressed in their khaki uniforms.

They had strange looks on their faces. They did not seem to have any physical wounds, but they looked different. Most of them were one-to-three years older than me, but you could tell that something was wrong with them.

We asked some of the fishermen on the wharf that was adjacent to the beach, what the Marines were doing here and what was wrong with them. The fishermen told us that in November, less than one month earlier, the Marine Corp invaded and captured a small coral atoll in the Pacific Ocean called Tarawa. Some of the casualties from that battle were recu-

Local State Guard Unit Prepared For Real Fight

California state guard units are being well trained as guerrilla fighters, in case the Japs should make a landing in California, with the camouflage unit of Company A, fourth battalion, thirty-third regiment, the San Jose unit, leading the way in their specialty.

Under the leadership of Cpl. Floyd L. (Chick) Glaze, World War I veteran who has been assigned the problem in guerrilla fighting, the unit is being well-schooled in Jap fighting.

Theoretically his squad becomes cut off from the main body and is forced into the hills to find protective covering and to live off the country while harassing the enemy.

To complete this mission skill in extended order, camouflage, woodcraft, scouting and setting booby traps is tested. The effectiveness of such training has been proven by regular troops fighting in the South Pacific.

Besides the camouflage group, all units of the state guard have regular assigned missions to accomplish in case California is invaded. The guardsmen have been training faithfully, and will give the Japs a bad time if they put in an appearance here.

Officers of Company A are Capt. L. C. Barnard, World War I veteran; First Lieut. M. Wright Emlen, and Second Lieut. Clifford Cummings.

San Jose Mercury News, 1942.

perating at the Casa Del Rey's R&R Center. Seeing this side of the realities of war made a strong impression on me.

When school started again after Christmas vacation, sitting in classrooms and playing football was not the primary thing on my mind. I felt that I had a responsibility to help in the war effort. I wanted to be a U.S. Marine.

I went to the Marine Corps Recruiting Office, gave the recruiter my name, address and telephone number, and told him that I was seventeen and wanted to enlist. The recruiter told me he needed proof of my age and my parent's signature.

Jack and Agnes Reding, August 1944.

Later that day the recruiter called my mother to obtain parental permission for me to join the Corps. She very firmly informed him that I was only sixteen years old. That ended my attempts in January 1944 to be a Marine. I would have to wait until August when I would be seventeen.

Even though my birthday was less than eight months away, at that time, it seemed like an eternity. I told my girlfriend that I was going to try to join the Marine Corps. She didn't want me to go into the military, but she understood and said she would wait for me.

CHAPTER II

YOU'RE IN THE NAVY NOW

On my seventeenth birthday, in the summer of 1944, I walked into my parent's bedroom at 7:30 in the morning. My dad worked the night shift and had just gotten to sleep.

I shook his shoulder and woke him up. I said, "Do you know what I want for my birthday?"

"What?" he responded in a sleepy, irritated voice.

"Your signature so that I can join the Marines," I said.

"You've got it," he responded.

My mother, who by then was wide-awake and had heard our conversation, said, "No! You can join the Navy, but not the Marines."

I said, "Okay, the Navy will be fine."

My mother told me to leave my father alone and let him get some sleep. Later that morning, after he got up, he said to me, "Let's go."

The Navy recruiting office was in the United States Post Office Building on North First Street across from St. James Park. But my birthday was on a Saturday—we found the office closed for the weekend. We would have to wait until Monday morning.

When the recruiters opened the doors on Monday morning, my dad and I were there waiting for them. I showed them my birth certificate and filled out the enlistment papers. My father showed the recruiters his identification and signed the parental consent form.

Reflecting back, it was a good thing that my mother insisted I go into the Navy rather than the Marine Corps. Most of the fellows that went into the Marines at that time ended up at Iwo Jima. If it weren't Iwo Jima, then it would have been Okinawa. I ended up there anyway, but fortunately as a sailor aboard a ship and not as a marine rifleman.

Jim and Jack Reding, just before Jim went into the Navy. 1944.

REPORTING FOR ACTIVE DUTY

Three weeks later, I reported for active duty at the San Jose Naval Recruiting Office. Thus began the journey to boot camp and the twenty-two months that would change my life.

Don Hutchinson, a friend from San Jose High School, also joined the Navy, and we reported for active duty together. It was nice to see him. We buddied up. It was reassuring to have someone I knew with me as I went off into the unknown.

After saying goodbye to my girlfriend and our parents, we "formed up" for the next step: transportation to boot camp. I did not mind leaving my parents but I was having second thoughts about leaving my girlfriend. I really liked her.

Our group was given instructions, and one of the older recruits was put in temporary charge of us. A petty officer from the recruiting office walked with us over to the Greyhound bus depot on South Market Street. At the bus station, we boarded a bus that took us on the fifty-mile ride up the Bayshore Highway (101) to San Francisco.

When we passed the naval air station at Moffett Field, we saw a Navy blimp approach its mooring for a landing near one of the large hangars.

As we got closer to San Francisco, we saw rows of new merchant "liberty" ships under construction. You could see the activity in the ship-yards. There was a bustle of movement, and brilliant flashes of light from the arc welders as large steel plates were being joined together.

San Francisco Bay and almost every dock along the San Francisco waterfront were filled with all kinds of vessels. There were aircraft carri-ers at the Alameda Naval Air Station and numerous types of warships anchored in the waters between Alameda and San Francisco. Freighters were located as far south as the small peninsula near San Mateo.

Our bus drove down Market Street toward the ferry building on the Embarcadero. We turned onto the Embarcadero and pulled up to the YMCA, which was and is still located on the northern side of the San Francisco–Oakland Bay Bridge.

The sidewalks along the waterfront were filled with a sea of white-hatted sailors going to and from their ships. San Francisco was a Navy town.

After we checked into the YMCA and were assigned our rooms, we gathered together for a meeting. We were told that there were two naval-recruit training stations located on the West Coast. One was in San Diego, California and the other was in Farragut, Idaho.

They said that recruits in drafts, or groups of fifty to one hundred men, would be sent to San Diego or Farragut depending upon the needs of the Navy. The next morning, after we were aboard the train, we would find out where we were going.

Don Hutchinson and I were assigned a room with two other new sailors. I wrote my folks a letter on the YMCA stationery. Since I was in the Navy, I didn't have to pay for postage to mail my letters. All I had to do was write my name, rank and military address in the corner of the envelope, and the word "FREE" where a stamp would usually go.

That night, I had trouble sleeping. There was so much to think about. I hoped I was doing the right thing . . . but it was too late now. I was excited. They said that boot camp was tough. I wondered if I would be able to meet the challenge.

If you didn't measure up to the Navy's mental and physical standards, they "washed you out" and sent you home. Maybe some of the reluctant draftees wanted to be returned to civilian life, but I wanted to go to sea.

Aside from my girlfriend, there wasn't much for me at home except the routine of attending high school. To say all of those goodbyes to go off to war, and then be sent home because you couldn't pass the mental or physical tests, would really be awkward and embarrassing.

We spent the night at the YMCA. Early the next morning after breakfast, we went outside and were formed up as a group into rows of three. Carrying our small travel bags, we walked down the Embarcadero to the Ferry Building. We boarded a Southern Pacific Railroad ferryboat for the approximate half-hour ride across the bay from San Francisco to Oakland.

In Oakland, we were taken to a troop train. The only civilians aboard were the crew. We were assigned to a Pullman sleeping car. The Porter patiently explained to us that we'd be heading north to Portland, Oregon, which was an overnight trip and that our seats could be made into beds.

Some of the men said that the train had started in Los Angeles. The San Diego Naval Training Station was only about a hundred miles south of Los Angeles. Why the Navy would send recruits from Southern California somewhere else for boot camp was a puzzlement.

As the troop train had proceeded northward along the coastal route to Oakland, they said it made periodic stops at cities and military bases along the way to pick up new recruits and troops.

The Navy petty-officer-in-charge of our group informed us that we were going to a base called Farragut, Idaho, which was located near Spokane, Washington. A naval recruit training station in Idaho? We didn't understand why the Navy would have a recruit training facility so far inland, and in—of all places—Idaho.

It was exciting. I'd never been on a train before. In the evening, the porter came around and made our seats into bunk-type beds. I got the upper bed. Trains were a nice way to travel. The sound of the wheels on the rails had a rhythm that put me to sleep.

The next morning we arrived in Portland. Our car was one of several that were connected to another train going northeast to Spokane. There we were transferred to a train with coach-type-cars. We traveled eastward to Coeur d'Alene, Idaho, then north to the small town of Athol.

From the train, we were herded aboard a large, enclosed, flatbed trailer pulled by the cab of a semi-truck. They called the trailer a cattle wagon. I could see why—we felt like livestock being moved from one area to another. Once aboard our makeshift bus, we proceeded on a slow bumpy five-mile ride from the train station to the Naval Training Center and the receiving barracks for our new home.

BOOT CAMP: UNITED STATES NAVAL TRAINING STATION, FARRAGUT, IDAHO

Upon our arrival at the training center a petty officer was there to greet us. He lined us up in rows and marched us in formation to a large wooden building where we were each assigned a bunk. From there we walked in formation to a large mess hall for the evening meal. Everything we did was in "formation." I was surprised that they didn't have us go to the bathroom in "formation."

After dinner, we made our own beds, or as sailors say, "sacks" or "racks" and were allowed some free time. I was exhausted. Most of us immediately went to bed (hit the sack). As soon as my head touched the pillow, I was sound asleep.

The next morning at 0530 hours (5:30 a.m. civilian time), we were awakened by the sounds of a bugle-playing reveille. A petty officer turned on the lights in the barracks and shouted for us to get up. After breakfast— or chow, as they said in the Navy—we went to another large building that was used to process incoming recruits.

At the processing center we were lined up alphabetically. My name is Reding and the fellow next to me was Pacheco. He was from Los Angeles. He had long hair that was his pride and joy. He kept combing it and looking at himself in every mirror around.

Apprehensively, we entered the large building to begin the transition from civilians to future sailors in the United States Navy. I was tired, excited and nervous.

We walked into a room lined with barber chairs. The first thing they did was to give us what they called a haircut . . . but it was actually a "head shear."

The barbers smiled when they saw Pacheco. When it was our turn,

Farragut, Idaho, 1944.

we sat down in the chairs, Pacheco next to me. As soon as we were seated, the barbers went to work with surgically quick movements. In a matter of moments, my hair was gone, and the barber was ready for the next recruit. I looked over at Pacheco. As his long hair fell to the floor, tears began to well up in his eyes. He held them back as he was transformed from an L.A. dandy to a U.S. Navy recruit. He was a nice guy, and we became friends. He would become a good sailor.

After receiving our haircuts, we began an assembly-line physical and dental examination. The culmination was, what seemed to me, a never-ending series of hypodermic needles in our arms to immunize us against typhoid, tetanus, small pox, diphtheria and diseases that I didn't even know existed. I felt like I'd just walked through a porcupine den. My body ached and my arms were sore for days. I wasn't alone. Most of the other fellows were as confused as I was and many of them commented about their sore arms.

From the medical line, we proceeded in single file to the supply line, where we received Navy uniforms (dungarees and "undress blues"—no stripes on the collar—for work, and dress uniforms—whites for warm weather and "dress blues" for temperate weather), blankets, a thin mattress and the other government-issue items that we would need to be sailors. All of the wool clothing had the unpleasant strong odor of mothballs.

We emerged from the other end of the building with sore arms, sheared heads, our bedding and new uniforms. Within three hours we had removed, packed and addressed our civilian clothes for shipment home, received our physicals and were issued the necessary clothing and gear for our transition from civilians to sailors. Confused and to a degree overwhelmed, we wondered what more they were going to do to us.

From the processing center, carrying all of our new, worldly possessions, we boarded buses that took us to our barracks—or as the Navy says, "quarters"—which would be our new home for the next ten weeks.

The training schedule was usually twelve weeks. At times it was accelerated to eight or ten weeks depending on the Navy's personnel requirements to man newly constructed ships or provide fleet replacements. Our normal, twelve-week schedule was compressed into ten weeks. During the process, they gave us aptitude and IQ tests.

Also, our entitlements were explained to us. An important one was a G.I. Life Insurance Policy for $10,000. The premiums were $5 per month, which could be deducted from our pay. They highly recommended that we take the policy, which I did, naming my parents as the beneficiaries. Ten thousand dollars was a lot of money. In early 1944, the parents of a friend purchased a nice, two-bedroom house on a large lot in San Jose for three thousand dollars. I figured if something happened to me, my folks would have enough money to move out of their small apartment and have a home of their own.

Part of our initial indoctrination informed us that Farragut Naval Training Center had from twenty to twenty-five thousand recruits going through the basic-training program. Also, that recruits were called "boots." The name came from the canvas leggings, or "boots," that new recruits were required to wear.

Most of the base was constructed in 1942. It was comprised of seven camps: Bennion, Gilmore, Hill, Peterson, Scott, Ward and Waldron.

All of the camps were named after deceased Naval personnel that had distinguished themselves in combat. Four of them were posthumously awarded the Congressional Medal Of Honor and one the Distinguished Service Cross.

Camps Waldron, Ward, Bennion, Hill and Scott were used as training facilities. Camps Gilmore and Peterson were used for post-recruit technical schools. The base also had a large naval hospital.

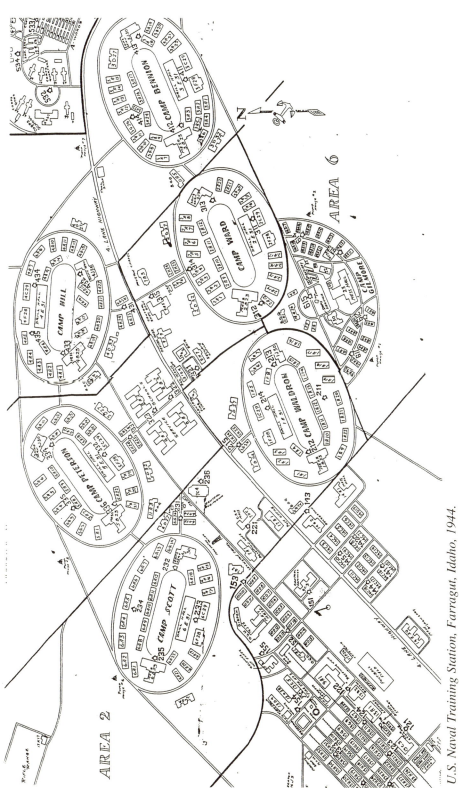

U.S. Naval Training Station, Farragut, Idaho, 1944.

The Naval Training Center had five regiments of recruits, one for each camp. Each regiment was comprised of twenty-two companies with from 100 to 150 men per company. This organizational structure resulted in a continuous flow of from 4,000 to 5,000 trainees per camp that were in the process of learning how to become sailors. The entire complex with its support personnel was like a city with a population of over 40,000 people.

The camps were laid-out in an oval shape around a fourteen-acre parade-ground- assembly area called the "grinder." To give you an idea of how large that would be: they said that over ten football fields—with spectator seats—would fit on our parade ground.

Around the perimeter of the grinder were the barracks where the recruits lived, a recreation hall, a medical dispensary for minor illnesses, and a huge drill hall so large that it resembled an airplane hangar.

As recruits, we were housed in two-story barracks, each holding two companies. Our "sacks" were wooden bunk beds. The conditions were crowded. This congestion was a test to see if we had the ability and temperament to adjust to the small, confined quarters that we would find aboard a United States Navy ship.

Whenever we went to sick call at the dispensary for a cold, or if we just didn't feel good, the pharmacist mate on duty would invariably give us the Navy's cure-all APC pill. The pharmacist mates said it meant "all-purpose capsule." This was before the modern-day miracle drugs like penicillin. I didn't know what it contained, but they dispensed it for almost every illness. Someone said it was just an aspirin tablet, but whatever it was, most of the time it did the job.

During the era of the Depression years (1930–1941) when money was scarce, most of the kids that I knew only went to the dentist when they had a toothache that wouldn't go away. If you had a cavity, you would put a clove in the hole in the tooth to help suppress the pain. For some reason, it worked. Personally, as a youngster and as a teenager, I can't remember going to the dentist except when I had a bad toothache or a broken tooth.

If a recruit required dental treatment, which most of us did, painkillers were used for only the most serious problems. If surgery or extractions were required—depending on the degree of difficulty—usually a colorless liquid anesthetic called ether would be used for sedation.

The dentist said that I had some cavities, which he later filled. For regular cavities, the patient sat in the dental chair and the dentist just started drilling. I can still smell the odor created by his drill. Amalgam fillings were put into the teeth with nothing to help relieve the intense discomfort caused when the instrument hit a nerve. Naval dental treatment was not for sissies.

For ten weeks, our entire world was within the confines of the base. Most of the training activities were held within the perimeter of our camp. Almost everything we needed—housing, food, classrooms, recreation center, physical education and medical facilities—was laid out around the oval world of our camp's grinder.

CAMP WALDRON

I was assigned to Company 876-44, Regiment 1, Battalion 3, in Camp Waldron. Our camp was named after a Navy pilot, Lieutenant Commander John Waldron, who was said to be part Sioux Indian. He was the commander of Torpedo Squadron 8 from the carrier USS *Hornet*. (CV 8).

On June 4, 1942, Commander Waldron's squadron of fifteen slow, cumbersome torpedo bombers took off from the *Hornet* to attack a Japanese carrier. They were told prior to takeoff that the enemy task force was one-hundred-seventy-five-plus miles away. The tanks on their pre-WWII aircraft held only enough fuel to fly approximately three hundred miles.

With the full knowledge that they were marginal on their fuel, Torpedo Squadron 8 proceeded on their mission to locate and sink the Japanese ships.

Commander Waldron and his squadron attacked the enemy fleet. In the face of withering Japanese anti-aircraft fire, they were all shot down. Only one pilot from the squadron of fifteen, Ensign George Gay, survived. Other Naval aircraft from our carriers continued the attack on the Japanese ships, sinking one of their cruisers and four of their carriers. Our fleet suffered the loss of one carrier, the USS *Yorktown* (CV 5). We had achieved our goal of stopping the aggressor with superior forces.

The Battle of Midway (as it was later called) was not only a naval victory; it also was a powerful psychological accomplishment. Prior to Midway, the Japanese had achieved relatively swift, easy victories over American military forces.

Starting with their attack on our fleet at Pearl Harbor on December 7, 1941, coupled with their successful military conquests at Guam, the Philippines Islands, China and the European Colonies in Southeastern Asia, the Japanese military felt superior and almost invincible.

Those victories led them to believe that Americans did not have the spirit or resolve to prevail in battle against the armed forces of the Imperial Japanese Empire. On that decisive day, the damage inflicted on the Japanese fleet by United States Naval aircraft helped to alter the course of the war.

The courage and sacrifice of our naval aviators demonstrated to the leaders of Japan that American military personnel, as warriors, had an inner resolve and determination to match or exceed any fighting force in the world.

The determined tenacity of the attack by Commander Waldron and his squadron of pilots was a contributing, pivotal, psychological turning point in the conflict. We were proud to be assigned to a camp named after Commander John Waldron.

At the time, we were unaware that our cryptologist had broken the Japanese Naval Code. This Top Secret knowledge allowed us to decipher their radio messages thus giving us a tactical advantage over their naval forces. This intelligence breakthrough was a major contributing factor for our success at Midway and other naval engagements in the Pacific.

COMPANY 876-44, REGIMENT 1, BATTALION 3

Our basic training company originally consisted of 120 men. Most of us were seventeen and eighteen years old. At that age, as future sailors, we were thereafter referred to as men and men we were expected to be. We lived up to their expectations. Our company was housed in an open-bay dormitory on the first floor of a two-story barrack building.

Some of the recruits had difficulty in learning how to adjust to the regimentation. Those who couldn't meet the required standards were sent home.

By the time we had completed the intense ten-week training program, only 100 men were left in our graduation class. Due to illness and for other reasons, twenty of the recruits who started with us did not complete the schedule with the rest of our group.

Our Company Commander, who was in charge of transforming us

from civilians into sailors, was Chief Petty Officer W. E. "Red" Garrett. He was our immediate commanding officer. With respect, we addressed him as "Chief" or "Sir."

Chief Garrett was firm, but he was fair. At thirty-four, he was twice as old as most of us—we considered him an old man. In civilian life, the Chief was a high school coach and physical education instructor from Alabama. The kids who had him in class had a good teacher. He was a nice guy and a positive leader. Some of the other outfits had company commanders with reputations of being mean and nasty. We were fortunate to have W.E. "Red" Garrett as our company commander.

For identification purposes, each company had a small white flag attached to a wooden pole. The flag was called a guidon. The company's number was prominently displayed on its white field. Our number was 876. Whenever we moved in formation, which was almost everywhere, the guidon bearer carried the small flag. He marched in front of the formation with the company commander or the non-commissioned-officer-in-charge (NCOIC).

For our parade drills and formation marching we were issued World War I vintage rifles. To me, carrying a flag on a pole seemed much better than carrying a rifle. As a member of the San Jose High School State Guard program, I'd learned the manual of arms rifle drills and formation marching. With this background, I applied to Chief Garrett to be the recruit responsible for carrying the company's flag. The chief gave me a tryout and accepted me for this important position.

Every day I was required to be parade sharp in my grooming, bearing, uniform and marching ability, because I was out in front of the formation. It was a challenging job. I liked being the guidon bearer.

In the Camp Waldron complex, we had two-story wooden barracks that were heated by coal-fired furnaces. As "boots," in two-man teams, we rotated the two-hour furnace watches. There was a large pile of coal located in a corner of the room. Working together using large flat-nosed shovels, we rhythmically fed (stoked) chunks of coal into the furnace to keep the fires burning.

That assignment was unpleasant duty. The air in the room was clouded with coal dust. On duty we wore our blue dungarees and dark knitted watch caps. By the time our watch was over, our faces and clothes would be covered with the black dust. No one ever mentioned anything about

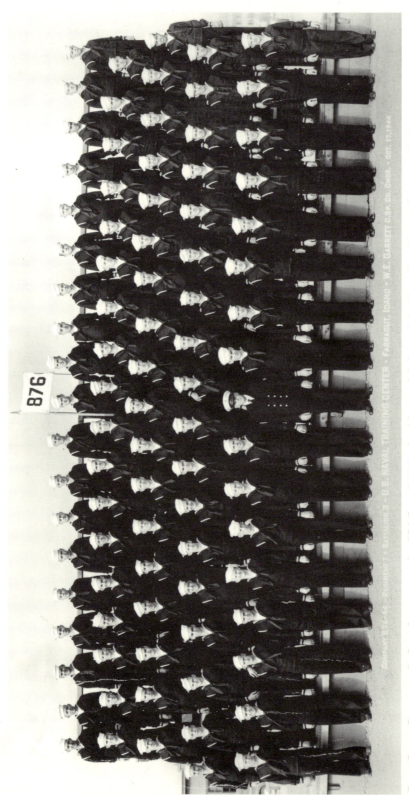

Boot Camp Company. Reding, last row, under 876 flag; R.V. Little, 4th row, 8th from right; Don Hutchinson, 1st row to left; Chief Garrett, 1st row, center.

COMPANY 876-44, REGIMENT 1, BATTALION 3

BOTTOM ROW (Left to Right)	SECOND ROW (Left to Right)	THIRD ROW (Left to Right)	FOURTH ROW (Left to Right)	FIFTH ROW (Left to Right)
Hutchison, D. C.	Heflin, H. F.	Rongey, R. J.	Kissling, I. C.	Leitner, T. J.
Branson, W. D.	Enochs, W. E.	White, R.	Schaefer, J.	Lanning, C. D.
Gragg, I. L.	Ford, R. E.	Bonner, T. W.	Taff, C. L.	Murray, L. W.
Wright, R.	Powell, B. L.	Pacheco, W. A.	Hazen, E. H.	Shoemaker, L. D.
Flickinger, M. L.	Stroud, J. M.	Garcia, B. G.	Pirtle, J. W.	Stephens, D. A.
Winihan, P. K.	Weiss, R. E.	Hepler, R. A.	Voss, J. W.	Watson, M. G.
Richardson, D. D.	Hardy, T. K.	Johnson, N. C.	Ivey, G. H.	Kinney, W. G.
Bolen, H. A.	Stearns, A. L. (Jr.)	O'Brien, G. P.	Schuuten, H.	Johns, A. D.
Garrett, W. E.*	Osbrink, R. L.	Chittenden, J. S.	Whitehurst, A. L.	Burgess, C. M.
Tremayne, D. H.	Moritz, B. A.	Kernohan, O. A.	LaCerte, G. D.	Reding, J. J.
Sauer, E. W.	Tullos, I. L.	Johnson, H. R. E.	Sellards, R. C.	Williams, J. B.
Hale, W. A.	Stenson, R. E.	Breuer, R. A.	Little, R. V.	Prock, S. C.
Martin, J. L.	Rowe, R. E.	Marpert, R. J.	Earle, G.	Leedom, R. L.
Sullivan, J. R.	Hopkins, J. R.	Passmore, C. L.	Baker, L. W.	Pasteris, E. M.
Jefferies, J. M.	Jameson, D. E.	Kramer, C. W.	Braver, E. W.	Neugbauer, M.
Clifford, L. H.	Emerson, D. H.	Jones, E. W.	Mathews, I. S.	Good, L. G.
Bottom, D. E.	Bishop, A. W.	Croker, J. E.	Brogdon, B. B.	Wylley, R. A.
	Sheppard, G. S.	Guzman, C. A.	Rainey, S. J.	Lough, W. W.
				Herting, H. R.

wearing any kind of protective breathing mask.

On piercing cold nights, you didn't dare let the fires die down. If you did, you'd have a couple of hundred unhappy fellow recruits from the two companies descend upon you. The furnace watch was hard work, but when your turn came, you stood your watch and did your job.

The daily training routine began at 0530 (5:30 a.m.) with the sound of a bugle being played over the camp's public address system to announce reveille. Our boot company learned how to work together. It took teamwork for over one hundred men in crowded conditions with limited facilities to shave, shower, make our bunks, police the barracks and fall out for morning formation in less than thirty minutes.

Once assembled, we would have morning roll call and then march in formation to the parade ground for up to an hour of physical-training exercises.

In that part of northwestern Idaho the weather could quickly change. Within a twenty-four hour period, we could have sunshine, rain, piercingly cold wind and even snow.

During inclement weather, we would march to the huge gymnasium on the perimeter of the parade ground. In the gymnasium, we'd assume our pre-assigned positions for morning exercises. We would do calisthenics and rifle drill exercises, many times to the accompaniment of music from the camp's Navy band.

It was really impressive when the entire regiment, consisting of from three to five thousand men, assembled on the parade ground. Having such a large formation of men exercising in unison to the music of the Navy band, or passing in review, was a spine tingling experience. Being a member of the Camp Waldron regiment gave me a strong sense of pride and belonging.

The singer and actress Lena Horne recorded a popular song entitled "Stormy Weather." We modified the lyrics to be:

Don't know why
There's no sun up in the sky,
Farragut weather . . .
Which keeps my gal and I from being together,
Cause it keeps raining all of the time,
The time,
Keeps raining all the time.

And did it rain! The weather was cold, wet and miserable.

The fellows who did their recruit training in San Diego were certainly fortunate to be in sunshine.

Another song, which was indelibly stamped into my mind, was "Humoresque." The camp's Navy band frequently played it when we did our morning rifle-formation exercises. I can still hear the refrain of the melody.

After morning exercises, we marched to the mess hall, commonly referred to as the chow hall, for breakfast. The camp's mess hall had the capabilities of feeding over two thousand at a sitting. Since our regiment had from four-to-five-thousand men, each meal required that we schedule our activities for either a first or second seating. Consequently, the schedule for our morning exercises and breakfast would be determined by our training activities for the day.

Monday through Friday after breakfast, when we'd completed our morning cleanup chores, we attended recruit-training classes. If we needed any booster immunization shots, we would receive them Friday morning. That same afternoon, we would have a "field day." Which meant that we would, with sore arms and aching bodies, give our barracks a clean-scrub-down "fore and aft." Whoever set up our grueling schedules was certainly short on sympathy.

Saturday mornings after personnel inspection, we pretty much had the rest of the day and Sunday off, unless we were scheduled to stand sentry duty or furnace watch.

During the ten weeks of boot camp, we received only one "liberty." That one was to Couer d'Alene, Idaho, which was located along the shore of a beautiful lake. The town was only about twenty miles south of the base. It had a main street with several bars and a movie theater. At the end of the street was a great community park with a nice lakeside beach.

Couer d'Alene was a friendly town that was crowded with white-hatted Navy recruits on their "boot liberty." About the only thing to do was to drink beer and go to the movies, which is what most of us did.

Beer was the beverage of choice for almost all of us. A glass of beer cost ten cents. In order to go into the bars, I took my shaved-head, recruit ID card and modified the year of birth to read 1923. That made me twenty-one years of age, which was old enough to buy a drink.

During the basic training program practically every boot company had several men become ill. The local Indians called the area where the training station was located Fever Valley. They must have known something that the Navy didn't, because they were right.

Recruits would come down with a fever that many times developed into either measles, mumps, pneumonia, strep throat, scarlet fever, rheumatic fever or even spinal meningitis. Almost every boot company was affected. Fever Valley was an appropriate name for the area.

If you became ill, required hospitalization and fell behind your company's training schedule by missing more than a few days, upon release from the hospital you'd be reassigned to a different company so that you could complete all of the phases of your training.

Some of the boots, due to illnesses and other factors, were unable to meet the strenuous demands of the training schedule. They were sent home. The program was designed to determine if you had the ability and temperament to live in confined, uncomfortable quarters, get along with strangers, endure rigorous hardships, and be able to work together as a member of a crew for long stressful hours under hazardous conditions. Injuries and fatalities did occur. We were being trained to fight a war for the survival of the nation.

BOOT LEAVE

Three weeks before we completed our training and graduated from boot camp, someone shaking my shoulder awakened me around 4:30 a.m. Standing next to my bunk was Mike Giansiracua, a fellow from my high school who was in the next barracks. In a whisper, he said he was leaving the base to go home on boot leave. Did I want him to call my parents? If so, what was their telephone number?

In the quiet of the pre-dawn darkness, I gave him my home telephone number. After he left, I tried to go back to sleep, but the thought of home got to me. For the first time in the seven weeks that I'd been in the Navy, I was homesick. With tears in my eyes, I quietly cried myself back to sleep.

Finally, after what seemed like an eternity, we completed our recruit-training program. Upon graduation, we were promoted from apprentice seaman with one stripe on the cuff of our sleeves to seaman second class with two stripes on the cuff of our sleeves. We also received a monthly pay increased from fifty dollars per month to fifty-four dollars per month. In other words our pay scale went from one dollar sixty-seven cents per

Ready to "Pass in Review," October 1944.

day to one dollar eighty cents per day. As Seaman Second Class, we could remove our canvas leggings thereby becoming "bell-bottom" sailors. Best of all, we received a ten days leave, which was enough time for us to go home for a visit.

Our graduation ceremony was memorable. I especially liked the pass in review parade where, in company formations, almost five thousand of us marched around the grinder to the music of the Navy band. It was too bad that my folks and my girl friend lived so far away. They would have enjoyed this special event. The tradition was, after the ceremony when the graduates went back to their barracks, each person in your company would sign each other's canvas "boot" leggings. I still have mine.

Early the next morning the cattle-car trailer carried us from the training center to the Athol Train Station. At the train station, the commuter train took us the fifty miles to Spokane, Washington. There, I caught the overnight train to San Jose, California and home.

My girlfriend was happy to see me, but it wasn't the same. Again, she said that she would wait for me but it wasn't fair to ask her. She was sixteen years old and a junior in high school. I'd had my seventeenth birthday less than three months earlier. She was going to school with all of its social activities, and I was going into the unknown. We agreed to write, but we did not make any commitment because I didn't know if, or even when, I would ever be home again.

In boot camp we had a planned structured routine. After being home for a few days I began to feel uncomfortable, out of my elements. I went

San Jose High School 1945 Yearbook. Bill Martin and Jim Reding, wearing white hats.

to my high school to see some of my former classmates. They were friendly and curious, but they seemed so young. They were high school students
and thought like sixteen-seventeen-and-eighteen year olds should think.
Even though I was the same age or even a year younger than many of
them, going through the intense training of boot camp had changed me.
We lived in different worlds. They were going to classes at a co-educa-
tional high school and I was going to war.

It was nice seeing my parents, friends and family. When my leave
was up, I was ready to return to Farragut, Idaho for my duty assignment.

Upon graduation from recruit training, we were given the opportunity to request a specialty school. Recruits with stronger educational back-
grounds scored higher on aptitude tests. They were the ones who seemed
to be selected to attend the specialty schools of their choice. I had left high
school after completing the first half of my junior year. There was so
much that I didn't learn or know about Math and English. I had requested
submarine school in New London, Connecticut, but was given sea duty
aboard a surface ship.

Reporting back to Farragut Naval Training station, I was assigned to
a "ship of the fleet" for sea duty.

CHAPTER III

SEA DUTY-RECEIVING SHIP, TERMINAL ISLAND

My orders were to report with bag and hammock to the receiving ship on Terminal Island, located between San Pedro and Long Beach, California for further assignment.

We departed from Farragut in a "draft" of fifty men. One of the sailors in our draft was R.V. Little. He had been with me in Company 876. We went through boot camp together. He was a quiet guy in his mid-to-late twenties, from Fort Worth, Texas. I think he was married and had a family. He was doing his duty, but for him the regimentation of military life was different.

Most of us were seventeen-or-eighteen-year-olds. We were still kids. We didn't have any family responsibilities. Because Little and the other older fellows had different interests, we didn't have much in common. He was a nice guy. Even though I never did get to know him very well, it was great to have someone I knew from my boot camp company going with me to the next duty station.

After a two-day train ride, we arrived in Los Angeles where we transferred to a bus that took us to San Pedro and the Terminal Island Naval Station. Sailors awaiting assignment to ships or to duty stations usually transitioned through receiving barracks. On Terminal Island we were temporarily quartered in one of these barracks, which was a huge, warehouse-type building containing several hundred bunks. The conditions were crowded and confusing.

I remained there for four days while my paperwork was being processed and my orders were cut assigning me to my ship, the USS *Fergus* (APA 82). "APA" meant that it was an "Amphibious Personnel

Assault" type of ship. "*Fergus*" was the name of the vessel, and "82" was its numerical identification. R.V. Little was also assigned to the same ship.

Those four days on Terminal Island were enlightening, because there was a naval prison located near the receiving barracks. The two facilities utilized the same large mess hall.

Every day we would see the Marine guards taking groups of inmates from the prison compound to the mess hall for chow. The prisoners would be formed up into squads, with guards at key positions around the perimeter.

The formations would be trotted at double time to the mess hall. If a prisoner got out of step, a guard would hit him with his nightstick. As the men went through the chow line, the guards were there to watch their every move.

When they sat down to eat, the first prisoners through the line would eat very slowly because when they were finished, all of the inmates were considered finished, and they were ordered out of the mess hall. In formation they would, again at double time, trot back to the prison compound. Watching the way these men were treated made an indelible impression on me.

Naval discipline was known for being swift and harsh. You followed the rules because you did not want to be incarcerated in a military prison. Maybe that was why the receiving ship was adjacent to one. They apparently wanted us to see what it was like to be an inmate. It made a believer out of me.

Desertion was one of the most severe acts of disobedience. It was defined as being "absent without leave" (AWOL). The most severe penalties were given to sailors that were AWOL and missed their ships when they sailed from the United States.

The 1943 Edition of the United States Navy's *Bluejacket's Manual* emphasizes the following code of conduct rules and regulations:

The punishment for desertion is a General Court Martial. The penalty in peacetime is very severe, usually a term of confinement amounting to years at hard labor in a naval prison.

In time of war the supreme penalty may be exacted—death. If a lesser punishment is meted out to an offender in time of war, it is always accompanied by loss of citizenship, a handicap that sticks throughout his natural life.

When a bluejacket has been "absent without leave" or "absent over leave" for more then twenty-four hours and has not communicated with his commanding officer giving reasons for his absence, a reward not exceeding twenty-five dollars is posted for the delivery of the straggler into the custody of naval authorities.

When a straggler is declared a "deserter," the reward is increased to fifty dollars for the apprehension and delivery of the deserter into the custody of naval authorities.

(At that time, I was making fifty-five dollars per month with "sea pay," so a fifty-dollar reward was a month's pay for a seaman.)

Offenses which may be punishable by death: Mutiny, disobedience of orders, striking a superior officer, dealings with the enemy, desertion in time of war, deserting trust in time of war, sleeping on watch, leaving station and duty before being regularly relieved, injuring a naval vessel or any part of her equipment, unlawful destruction of public property, treacherously yielding to an enemy when engaged in battle, cowardice in battle, deserting duty in battle and murder.

We were at war, and the Navy was serious. We had a few fellows who were habitually breaking the rules, but I don't remember anyone receiving a General Court Martial. Most of the troublemakers received "Captain's Masts." Which meant that they would usually be sentenced to solitary confinement for ten to fifteen days in the brig on bread and water (they were allowed to receive one full meal every third day), plus demotion in rank and loss of pay during the period of incarceration.

To be alone for ten to fifteen days, locked in a small, steel cell near the bottom of a rolling, tossing ship, caught your attention. Compounding the confinement, at any moment the ship could be hit by a torpedo or a floating mine.

Aboard our ship, the *Fergus*, an armed (Marine) guard was on duty twenty-four hours a day outside the cells, to make sure the prisoners fulfilled their sentences. In the event that the ship was under attack, struck a mine or was in any type of imminent danger, the guards were instructed to unlock the steel cell doors to the brig and escort the prisoners topside.

When I was a mess-cook, I frequently drew the assignment of bringing bread and, when allowed, a full ration of food to the prisoners. I would always give them extra food and make sure that there was a candy bar or some pastry with the meals. We were not supposed to give them extra food or desserts, but as long as it was not too obvious, no one said anything. We never mentioned the extras to the marine guards because they were serious. They seemed to have little sympathy for the prisoners.

I don't remember hearing of any Sailors, Marines or

Coastguardsmen being sentenced to death, but there was talk throughout the fleet of a soldier in Europe who had been executed for desertion.

ATTACK TRANSPORTS (APAS)

At the beginning of the war, troops were transported on large, former ocean liners and Army transport ships designated as APs. Also, the Navy pressed smaller coastal and inter-island passenger ships into service. Later, some of the smaller ships were refitted with davits to hold and launch landing crafts.

As the war progressed, we developed the tactic of transporting and landing thousands of troops, with their combat equipment, onto hostile shores. For this type of operation, a new type of troop ship was developed. This specialized ship was classified as an "amphibious personnel assault" (APA), or "attack transport."

These ships—depending upon their class and size—were capable of carrying anywhere from 600 to 1,500 combat troops and their equipment to foreign shores, and landing them on enemy beaches. A maximum effort was made to construct these much-needed vessels.

GILLIAM-CLASS APAS

There were thirty-two Gilliam-class APAs built in 1944. Each ship had two smokestacks, and was frequently referred to as a twin stacker. Their numbers were APA 57 to 88.

The Gilliam-class APAs were named after communities (counties) that had made substantial contributions to the War Bond drives. The USS *Fergus* (APA 82) was named after Fergus County, Montana. It was built in San Pedro, California.

This type of ship was considered a shallow drafted vessel because when fully loaded, its hull only went 15' 6" below the water line. The primary task for these transports was to carry combat personnel and their equipment "in close" (within one mile) to invasion landing beaches.

When we were in harm's way, we usually had destroyers, destroyer escorts or larger-size warships accompanying us to provide anti-submarine and anti-aircraft protective firepower.

Even though we were transports, we still had a cannon (naval cannons are referred to as guns) and several anti-aircraft weapons strategically located on the main deck and the superstructure of our ship.

The cannon was located on the flat open area at the rear of the main deck (the fantail). The weapon was designated as a 5 inch 38, which meant that the length of the barrel was 16 feet. The calculations used to determine the length of the barrel are as follows: 5 inches times 38 equals 190 inches. Divide by 12 (12 inches to a foot) to get 15.84 feet. Rounded, it equals 16 feet.

Our 20-mm and 40-mm anti-aircraft guns were on the port and starboard sides of the main deck and the superstructure. For a troop transport, we had credible firepower to defend ourselves against attacking aircraft and coastal-type vessels.

The ships were 426 feet in length with a beam (width) of 58 feet. They were powered by two turbo-electric engines with twin screws (propellers). The standard speed was sixteen knots and the flank (fastest) speed per hour was 18 to 20 knots.

The ship's displacement ("light" or when empty) was 4,100 tons. The carrying capacity was up to 2,700 tons counting the troops and their combat cargo. The displacement with the ship fully loaded was 6,800 tons.

Including the boat crews, the ship's company for the Gilliam Class APAs consisted of 37 officers and 270 enlisted men. Also, assigned were a marine detachment of one officer and six to twelve enlisted men. The Marines were in charge of the troop passengers.

When we were "combat loaded," the total members of the crew, including marines, was 43 officers and 287 enlisted men, plus 600 to 700 troop passengers, for a total of over one thousand men aboard ship.

The troops were berthed on the decks below the hatches over the number one ("forward" or front) and the number two ("aft" or rear) holds. The troops slept in sections. Their bunks, which were called sacks, were stacked in sets of four. Or, as we said aboard ship, the sacks for the troops were four tiers high.

The twin stackers were also secondary hospital ships. The ship's company medical detachment included a surgeon, a dentist and other medical personnel. The primary combat mission of the medics was to provide basic, life-sustaining care for wounded and injured personnel.

COMBAT LOADED TRANSPORT

U.S.M.C. HULL Nº   U.S. NAVY HULL Nº
U.S. MARITIME COMMISSION
WEST COAST REGIONAL OFFICE, OAKLAND CALIFORNIA

BUILT BY
CONSOLIDATED STEEL CORP., LTD.
WILMINGTON   CALIFORNIA

U.S.M.C. BLDR	U.S.N.	NAME
1881	751	APA 88	U.S.S PRESIDIO
1880	750	APA 87	U.S.S. NIAGARA
1879	749	APA 86	U.S.S GENEVA
1878	748	APA 85	U.S.S GASCONADE
1877	747	APA 84	U.S.S. GARRARD
1876	746	APA 83	U.S.S. FILLMORE
1875	745	APA 82	U.S.S FERGUS
1874	744	APA 81	USS FALLON
1873	743	APA 80	USS ELKHART
1872	742	APA 79	U.S.S DAWSON
1871	741	APA 78	U.S.S CULLMAN
1870	740	APA 77	U.S.S. CRITTENDEN
1869	739	APA 76	U.S.S. CRENSHAW
1868	738	APA 75	U.S.S CORTLAND
1867	737	APA 74	U.S.S. COLUSA
1866	736	APA 73	U.S.S CLEBURNE
1865	735	APA 72	U.S.S CLARENDON
1864	734	APA 71	U.S.S. CATRON
1863	733	APA 70	U.S.S CARTERET
1862	732	APA 69	U.S.S CARLISLE
1861	731	APA 68	U.S.S BUTTE
1860	730	APA 67	U.S.S BURLESON
1859	729	APA 66	U.S.S. BRULE
1858	728	APA 65	U.S.S BRISCOE
1857	727	APA 64	U.S.S BRACKEN
1856	726	APA 63	U.S.S BLADEN
1855	725	APA 62	U.S.S BERRIEN
1854	724	APA 61	U.S.S. BARROW
1853	723	APA 60	U.S.S BANNER
1852	722	APA 59	U.S.S AUDRAIN
1851	721	APA 58	U S S. APPLING
1850	720	APA 57	USS. GILLIAM

HULL NUMBERS

List of Twin Stackers, all constructed in 1944.

Twin stacker APA with guns and LCVP Boats.

THE BOATSWAIN'S PIPE

Aboard United States Naval Ships, the issuance of verbal orders is preceded by the shrill command whistle known as the "boatswain's pipe" (pronounced bos'n).

The pipe is an instrument of authority, which is almost always attached to a white, decorative halyard, and worn—with pride—around the duty boatswain's neck.

From known history to the Crusades, the heritage of the pipe goes back to the year 1248. In the fifteenth century, the duty boatswains on the warships of the British Navy wore the pipe as a prestigious instrument of honor.

In the 17th century, the British referred to it as a "call." The United States Navy commonly refers to the command whistle as a "boatswain's pipe."

On our ship, the more common calls which were piped by the duty boatswain over the ship's public address system were: All Hands (attention); Mess Gear (chow down—meal call); Boat Call (piped to "Away All Boats"); and Sweepers (man your brooms, clean sweep, down fore and aft. In other words, clean the ship).

LANDING CRAFT

We had fourteen landing craft aboard the *Fergus*. Thirteen were known as Higgins Boats, or Landing Craft Vehicle Personnel (LCVPs), or (VP's). They were 36 feet long, with a beam of ten feet and a draft was three feet aft and two feet forward. They were launched from four sets of davits, two sets on either side of the ship.

A LCVP was capable of carrying 36 to 40 troops with their combat back packs and weapons, but a more practical and realistic number would be 20 to 30 troops—depending upon the amount of gear they were taking ashore.

Seafarers have traditional titles for the men handling specific tasks aboard ships. The coxswains ("coxsuns") usually were in charge of the small boats carried on a ship. They manned the helms and determined the speed and direction of the boats.

The bow-hooks took care of the forward area of the boats and were responsible for handling the lines and the forward davit hooks. Also they were responsible for lowering the ramps when the boats hit the beach. The

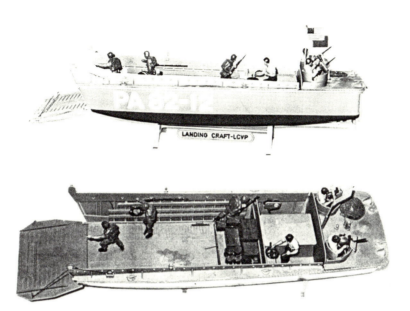

LCVP "Higgins" boat.

motor-macs kept the engine running. The stern- hooks handled the stern lines and the aft davit hooks.

In non-combat conditions, boat crews usually consisted of a coxswain, a motor-mac and a bow-hook. In combat, a fourth member of the crew was added to handle the stern-hook.

Communication between the ship and other boats was by a combination of a battery-powered backpack type radio, hand signals, blinker lights and signal flags.

The aft (rear) section of each boat contained two openings, or wells, that were originally incorporated into the boat's design as mounts for two fifty-caliber machine guns. I don't remember ever seeing guns mounted on the boats used in any of our operations.

Under normal sea and surf conditions, with the boats bobbing on the ocean's surface and being tossed around by the waves, the machine guns would had been more of a hazard than an asset.

In addition to the twelve LCVP's on the four davits (three boats per davit), we also carried one on the aft hatch over the number two hold. On the forward hold, we had a Landing Craft Personnel (LCP). For landing operations the LCP was usually assigned as the beachmaster's command boat. Under non-combat conditions, the captain used the LCP as his own personal boat. Then it was referred to as the Captain's Gig.

CONDITION ONE ABLE

"Set Condition One Able" was the command that the captain issued to begin the process of disembarking the troops and landing them on hostile beaches. Upon receipt of the order, the crew and troops went to their respective battle, boat-launching and assembly-point stations.

It took about three minutes for our crew to have our Condition One Able stations manned and ready. This meant that all of our guns were manned, the troops were in their pre-assigned assembly areas, and the boat crews were standing by their boats.

To capitalize on the cloak of darkness, many of the landings were initiated at the first light of dawn. When our captain issued the command "Away All Boats"—which meant launch your boats—the ship's company sprang into a flurry of action. Each boat's four-man crew was either in, or standing by, their boats. Almost in unison, from the four davits, the boats—with their crews aboard—would be lowered the 20 to 30 feet to the water.

Large heavy-duty hooks were attached to steel cables on booms connected to the masts over the number one and two hatches. These hooks would be attached to the manned LCP boat, or the LCVP boat. The boom operators, with a light, decisive touch, would gently yet quickly pick up the boats and lower them into the water.

Launching and retrieving the boats under normal daylight conditions was a hazardous operation, but in the darkness of the hours before dawn, the margin for error was compounded. Timing was critical for a successful launch or pickup. The davit operators would skillfully lower the boats into the water. Once in the water, with their engines roaring, the coxswains would steer their landing crafts to pre-assigned circle formations that would be off the port and the starboard sides of the stern of the ship.

Aboard the *Fergus* we had four debarkation stations. They were adjacent to the number one and the number two holds. Two of them were on the port and two were starboard sides of the ship.

As the boats were forming their circling patterns off the stern of the ship, the deck crews would place an 8 by 20-foot manila hemp rope cargo net at each troop debarkation station. One end of the cargo netting would be securely fastened to the ship, and the other end rolled over the railing so that it hung down to the water line.

Upon receipt of the order to "Commence loading your troops," the coxswains, would break from their circling formations and move their boats in single-file to pre-assigned loading areas. There they would idle their engines as the bow and stern-hooks pulled the netting into their boats.

Our Ship's Company Marines were in charge of the passengers. Coordinating with the troop's commanders, the Marines would have the men divided into sections, or squads. They would be held in their berthing quarters until called topside for debarkation.

In this electrified atmosphere, contrary to the Hollywood movies, there was very little talking among the troops. Most of them quietly listened for orders and instructions.

When their turn came they assembled on deck by squads near their debarkation stations. By then the landing crafts were alongside the ship with the nets pulled down into the boats. Upon command, in sets of three with combat gear on their backs and weapons on their shoulders, they would climb over the ship's railings and down the rope netting into the bobbing boats.

The troops were spaced so that there would be three sets of three on the netting. When the first set was halfway down, the next set would go over the side, so there was a continual flow during the debarkation process. They were cautioned to hold onto the vertical rather than the horizontal portion of the rope netting. If they held onto the horizontal part of the rope, they could have the climber above them step on their hands.

Loading troops into LCVP boats was dangerous. The degree of danger was dependent upon the wind, the size and surge of the waves, and the overall conditions of the operation. I don't remember our ship ever losing a man overboard or having someone injured during those delicate amphibious-loading procedures.

After the troops and their combat cargo were aboard the boats, the coxswains would drive their VP boats away from the ship and form their pre-assigned circular formations, or "waves." The holding patterns were in visual communication distance of their ship.

When the order was given by the Task Force Commander to "Land

Your Troops," each ship would then notify their boats to "Commence the Attack." The boats would then break from their circular holding patterns, move into their pre-assigned combat wave positions, and proceed towards their designated landing areas.

The wave commander at the mid-point of the formation would aim his boat at a dye marker or smoke pot that had been dropped into the water ahead by a destroyer or a destroyer escort. The marker would indicate the "point of attack" for that segment of the invasion landing force.

When his boat reached the marker, the wave's commander would give the signal for the coxswains to "Land Your Troops." Upon receipt of the order, each coxswain would push the throttle of his boat forward to flank (maximum) speed.

He was then on his own to drive his boat through the surf, over, around or through any obstacles or hostile opposition and land his troops along with their equipment at the designated landing area on the enemy's beach. It was like an aquatic cavalry charge.

The LCVPs were designed to operate with two feet of water forward and three feet of water aft. This shallow draft enabled the coxswains to drive their boats up as close to the shoreline as they could. Once in position, they would drop their ramps to disembark their troops or equipment. The moment the ramp was lowered, the troops would quickly leave the boat and move up onto the beach. Under hostile conditions, if there were wounded in the landing area, they would be loaded into the boats. The coxswains would then back their boats down through the surf, turn them around and return to the ship for another load.

This operation required considerable seamanship by the entire crew. In a high surf, it was not uncommon to have a boat "broach" (get caught sideways in a wave pattern, and capsize). During training exercises, we had several boats broach, and some crewmen were injured.

Once off the beach, the boats would turn around in the surf area and head back to their ship. Upon arriving, the boats would pull alongside where the wounded would—as gently as possible—be lifted up to the deck. Healthy troops that were returning to the ship would climb up the rope cargo netting.

USS *FERGUS* (APA 82)

I went aboard the *Fergus* as a member of the ship's company "commissioning crew." The *Fergus* was brand new, just out of the shipyard. Our captain was Commander J. C. Snyder, from Cynwyd, Pennsylvania. The Executive Officer was Lt. W. G. Morrison, from Jacksonville Florida. Being a member of the commissioning crew was special. We were known as plank owners, and this was our ship.

Most of the enlisted members of the crew had only been in the Navy for less than a year and over fifty percent of us had never been to sea before. A majority of the lower-level enlisted men were seventeen to nineteen years of age. There were so many of us seventeen-year-olds on the ships of the fleet that the old salts smilingly referred to us as "diaper sailors."

A nucleus of experienced officers and petty officers was the foundation of our ship's company. They did a remarkable job of molding us into a smoothly functioning unit. We quickly adapted to the shipboard routine, learned our jobs and became combat ready.

CENSORSHIP

When we reported aboard the *Fergus*, at our first division meeting our officers emphasized the importance of strictly following the rules and regulations regarding censorship. We were under specific restrictions as to what could and could not be disclosed. The rules were outlined in reminder posters, which were strategically located on ships and bases throughout the world. The posters basically said:

1. Censorship is common sense. Most of you do not need regulations. But you and your ship do need protection against the few careless or disloyal persons who can give the enemy the information needed to destroy you. To whom harmful information is addressed doesn't matter. It may never reach its destination. Tokyo or Berlin would be equally pleased with information addressed to your mother or to them.
(a) Mail all your letters aboard ship or on your station.
(b) Determine your proper address and use it.
(c) Don't use private codes.
(d) Remember that news stories and magazine articles and radio broadcasts of a military nature have been officially cleared for release. This does not give naval personnel permission to discuss

Officers: Captain Snyder, 1st row, center; Boatswain Caro, standing 8th from the right.

Chief Petty Officers: left to right: Dobier, Beavers, Edwards, Henningsen, Gunselman.

2nd Division: Reding, 1st row, 3rd from left; Schular has dog; R.V. Little, standing 2nd from right; Mr. Loutzennisea, Divsion Officer, standing center.

1st Division: McGinnis, last row, 5th from the right.

S Division. Eggebrecht, standing, 4th from the right.

C Division.

O Division. Mr. Cummins, Chief Edwards, back row.

Medical Division. Dr. Cazan, back row, center.

C & R Division.

E Division.

in detail the same or related incidents in unofficial, personal letters.

(e) International telephone calls, cables, and radiograms should be discussed in advance with your censor. Complying with certain details relating to these types of communications is required.

(f) Don't keep a diary and don't mail pictures of ships, planes, guns or other military equipment. Personal recordings are not permitted to be sent to or from naval personnel.

2. Follow the letter and spirit of these simple rules and you will have nothing to fear from the censor or from sneak-attacks from the enemy.

3. Below are listed a number of topics that are not permitted in private correspondence, cables or telephone conversations:

(a) The location, identity or movements of ships (naval or merchant), aircraft, or military personnel.

(b) The defensive or offensive forces, weapons, installations or plans of the United States or her Allies.

(c) Munitions or the location or progress of war industries.

(d) The routine or employment of any naval or military unit of the United States or her Allies.

(e) The effect of enemy operations or casualties until released.

(f) The criticism of equipment, physical conditions or morale of the United States or Allied forces.

(g) Any matter that might benefit the military, economic, or financial interests of the enemy or interfere with the war office or foreign relations of the United States or her Allies.

(h) Detailed descriptions of weather conditions.

Under wartime conditions, one of the first instructions we received from our petty officers prohibited us from keeping a personal diary or a log aboard our ship. The ship's wartime movements and activities were classified and considered confidential. Anyone caught with a diary would be subject to disciplinary actions that might even result in a Court Martial. The motto we were to follow was, "A Slip of the Lip Might Sink a Ship."

As a seventeen-year-old, I diligently followed orders. But after the war was over in August 1945 and censorship was lifted, I started keeping a diary of where we were and where we were going.

Also, several decades after the war was over, when the Ship's Log was declassified, I requested and received a copy of it from the Navy

Department. Through a collection of letters to my mother, the ship's news-papers and radiograms, plus talking to former shipmates during reunions, I began to piece together the following information about my time aboard the *Fergus*.

GOING TO SEA

While our ship was being completed, for training purposes we were sta-tioned aboard a sister ship, the USS *Braken* (APA 64). On the training ship, we went to sea under combat conditions to learn seamanship, emergency procedures and gunnery. The weapons we fired were 20-mm and 40-mm anti-aircraft guns and the 5 inch 38 cannon on the fantail of the ship.

Each week the *Braken* would leave San Pedro's Terminal Island Harbor to participate in naval maneuvers with other ships of the fleet in the waters off the coast of Southern California. We spent a lot of time sail-ing in and around the Channel Islands. Our days were filled with standing watches and learning seamanship duties, in conjunction with emergency drills and gunnery. We would fire the ship's guns at targets towed by air-craft, and at land-based object on one of the islands. I think its name was Santa Rosa Island.

When we passed within sight of another channel island named Santa Catalina, we were able to clearly see the land through the ship's powerful binoculars. Nestled in a cove was a small, picturesque town with a beach.

The settlement on the shores of the cove was Avalon, a little seaside resort community. It had homes that crawled up the hillsides above the water. They told us that before the war, Catalina had been a favorite hide-away for Hollywood movie stars and tourists from all over the country.

Located on the northern side of the cove is a famous ballroom dance hall. It is a large interesting domed-shaped building. With its palm trees and small beach, Avalon was, and still is, a picturesque seaside resort.

I wished that we could have pulled into the harbor and have gone ashore, but I understood that there was a coast guard training facility near the ballroom. The residents of Catalina didn't need any more sailors on their island.

WATER RATIONING

Fresh water aboard ships—especially at sea—was a precious com-modity. In port we received our fresh water supplies from barges or large hoses from the docking areas. This water was transferred into our holding tanks in the hull of the ship. At sea, our tanks would be replenished by evaporators, which were connected to our engine room powering system.

Drinking water was always available for all personnel. When we had troops aboard, usage for other purposes was restricted. Due to the size of our crew and the large number of passengers we carried on our ship, "water hours" were established. With the exception of showering and washing clothes, fresh water would then be allowed for the general usage of the ship's company and the passengers,

Otherwise, the troops and the crew took salt-water showers. Seawater was pumped from the ocean into an alternate system of pipes for showers and flushing the toilets. When taking a saltwater shower, a special strong, abrasive, soap was used to produce a cleansing lather. After taking one of those showers, there was an unpleasant, residual feeling of salt on your skin.

When we didn't have passengers aboard ship, more liberal freshwater hours were made available for crew showering. Even then, we would be restricted to taking a brief "Navy shower." Which meant you would turn the water on, rinse yourself down, turn the water off, soap yourself thoroughly, turn the water back on and rinse off.

Aboard ship, freshwater "Navy showers" were available daily for cooks, bakers, food handlers, medical personnel and the officers. Those showers were one of the premium benefits received by ship cooks.

When we were ashore and facilities were available with an ample supply of fresh water, one of the simple luxuries in life was to stand under a nice, warm shower for a long time.

Aboard ship, the restroom facilities are called heads. They were usually adjacent to the living quarters. The heads had open-bay showers in one corner of the compartment. The washbasins and mirrors for shaving were mounted on a wall separating the toilet facilities. These consisted of two large metal troughs with constantly flowing salt water to keep them clean. One was a stand-up urinal, and the other was at sitting height. It had six to ten wooden seats evenly spaced on the top. There was no privacy separation at either of the facilities. If you had any degree of modesty, you soon lost it aboard a U.S. Navy troopship.

OFFICERS' COUNTRY

Aboard most of the ships that sail the oceans and seas of the world, officers have the best accommodations that can be provided—considering the circumstances. Even the smaller vessels have a separate living area for officers.

On United States naval vessels, in addition to the extra space and more comfortable quarters, the only restrictions they had regarding the use of fresh water was what the captain imposed upon them. On the *Fergus*, the usage restriction was voluntary.

Aboard most Navy ships, they lived in a world of their own. Compared to the enlisted men, they had an elitist lifestyle. It was like the medieval feudal system of lords and peasants. Aboard our ship, they had a defined living area reserved for themselves. This separated section of the ship was called "officers' country." It was located amidship, above the main deck in the area known as the superstructure.

Their room assignments were according to their rank. The higher ranks received more spacious accommodations. The captain had a stateroom with a bed. Ensigns would have six to eight bunks in their compartment and so forth. All of the bunks had soft mattresses. Also, in each room there was a small desk for reading or writing.

They had a separate galley and eating facility called the wardroom. On our ship, the wardroom contained a large table, which could comfortably sit fifteen to twenty. It was used primarily for meetings and dining. When used for dining, it was covered with a linen tablecloth. The napkins also were linen and the eating utensils were silverware and china.

Their private galley had mess stewards that were specially assigned to cook for them and serve their meals. The mess stewards were usually of Filipino or African extraction. They received an extra five dollars per month pay for this sought-after duty.

The officers were on the same ship with the rest of the crew, but our lifestyles were a world apart. I tried to stay away from them—out of sight, out of mind. My contact with them was limited to when I stood bridge watches or during inspections.

The only one that I was comfortable talking to was Mr. Cummins. He was a former language professor at an East Coast University. He taught an English class aboard our ship for members of the crew who hadn't finished high school. I took his class. He encouraged us to go on to college after we completed our tours of duty in the Navy. Mr. Cummins was a gentleman. He had a positive directional influence on my life.

ENLISTED MEN'S QUARTERS

On the other side of the coin, the enlisted men in the Navy lived in poorly ventilated, crowded quarters in the hull of the ship. This was before the era of air-conditioning. Below deck, our primary source of fresh air was from vents and blowers. Also, spotted throughout the ship were small fans that were attached to the bulkheads (walls) to help circulate the hot stale air.

On some of the pre-war ships of the line, lower grade enlisted men slept on hammocks that were lashed (tied) to metal hooks in the ceiling and walls of large open areas or bays. During the day they would be taken down or lashed out of the way. The area could then be used for other purposes. During the war, hammocks were part of the gear that "boots" were issued in recruit training.

The surge of wartime shipbuilding contributed to the upgrading of living conditions for the enlisted personnel. Bunk beds were designed into newly constructed vessels. When the old-line warships were modified and brought up to date, bunks, which were more commonly referred to as "sacks" or "racks," were also incorporated into the upgrades.

The bunks that we had aboard the *Fergus* for the enlisted crew and passengers were made of oval metal pipe and hung from metal chains. A canvas base for holding the mattress was lashed to the metal pipe. On the canvas base we laid our small mattresses and bedding. I pressed my clothes by folding them neatly and placing them between the canvas and the mattress. The weight of my body lying on the mattress did a pretty good job.

The metal chains allowed the "sacks" to be tilted up and attached to the bulkheads. This was especially useful space-wise when we had a full compliment of crew and troops aboard. These "racks" were usually four tiers high.

In the cooks and bakers compartment, we had sixteen bunks. They were grouped into four sets. Each set was four-tiers-high. Personal privacy was almost non-existent.

Everyone seemed to have an individual preference. The location of your "sack" might seem like a little thing to make a big deal about. Aboard ship your own personal space was really limited. Therefore, your bunk became very important because it was yours. You spent a lot of time there.

Personally, I never wanted the bottom "sack;" guys would sit on them when they were sitting around shooting the bull. The top two were difficult to climb up into, and the air up there was warmer than the lower bunks. The next to the bottom bunk was my preference. It was easy to climb into and easy to make.

SHIPBOARD DUTY

When I reported aboard the *Fergus*, I was assigned to the Second Division of the deck force. Our job was to maintain the aft portion of the ship and to stand watches. Being a crewmember aboard a US Navy ship is a demanding seven days a week, twenty-four hours a day job to be performed under all kinds of weather and conditions.

My primary duties as a deck hand were chipping paint and painting, handling lines, splicing rope and standing watches. With the rank of seaman second class I was required to do any other shipboard emergency and non-emergency assignments that may be necessary for the operation and safety of the ship.

The enlisted men were divided into two basic groups, the "right-arm rates" and the "left-arm rates." In the old Navy—depending upon your job—the insignia of your rank would be located on your right or left arm.

A non-rated sailor either had a white stripe on his right shoulder, which basically designated that he worked topside, or a red stripe on his left shoulder indicating that he was part of the engine gang.

Petty officers such as cooks, bakers, pharmacist mates, radiomen and machinist mates that had jobs located primarily in the interior of the ship had their rank insignia sewed on their left arm. They were referred to as left-arm rates.

Right-arm petty officer rates were located topside. These were your boatswain mates (deck force and boat crews), gunner's mates, quartermasters and signalmen. The right-arm rates generally considered themselves to have the more glamorous, macho jobs on the ship. Today all petty officers rate and rank insignias are located on their left arm.

As part of my on-the-job training for the deck force, I was sent to Point Mugu at Port Hueneme for gunnery school. At Point Mugu, we learned the gun crew positions and practiced firing the weapons (the 20-

mm and 40-mm anti-aircraft guns plus the 5 inch 38 cannon), which we had aboard our ship. When I returned to the *Fergus*, my general quarters assignment was as an ammunition handler or as a loader on a twin-barrel 40-mm anti-aircraft gun.

DAWN AND DUSK ALERTS

At sea, a ship was most vulnerable from air and submarine attack at dawn, dusk and on moonlit nights. If we were in a war zone or in harm's way, we would be at our battle stations one or more hours before dawn and sometimes one hour before sunset.

The General Quarters (GQ) alarm would be sounded for the Dawn Alert at 0400 (4 a.m.). Depending upon our latitude and the month of the year, we would remain at our battle stations until after sunrise which would be from 0545 to 0655 (5:45 a.m. to 6:55 a.m.).

The evening GQ-Dusk Alert—would be in the late afternoon until the sun had set and the night helped to hide us with its protective cloak of darkness. Most of the time we just had Dawn Alerts unless we were in an area with a high possibility of imminent attack. Then we would also go on Dusk Alerts.

BOW WATCH

North of the equator the Pacific Ocean currents basically move in a clockwise direction. These currents reportedly travel at a speed of about three knots per hour. Depending upon the weather and other conditions, mines adrift in the waters off the coast of Japan could end up floating in the waters off the coast of Washington, Oregon or California.

One of the reasons why the US Navy had such a relatively low incident of ships striking floating mines was because our sailors stood "bow watches." The bow lookout duty station was manned twenty-four hours per day. The sailor wore a headset with a microphone strapped to his chest. The microphone was positioned so that he could easily push the activation button to relay information to the bridge or Combat Information Center (CIC).

The in-port bow watch was responsible for checking the anchor or the mooring lines to make sure that all lines were secure and the anchor —if used—was holding. Also, he had to be aware of anything that could be a danger to the safety of the ship or its crew.

At sea, his job was to look for mines, the periscope of a submarine, and an aircraft on the horizon or anything that could be an obstruction to navigation or a danger to the ship.

The standard length of time for these duty assignments was four hours. Exceptions to the four-hour rotation schedule were the night "dog watches" from 0000 hours to 0200 hours, (midnight to 2:00 a.m.) and 0200 hours to 0400 hours (2:00 a.m. to 4:00 a.m.). Those duties were for two hours because, at reveille, the men that stood the "dog watches" were still required to wake up with the rest of the ship's company and do their regular workday jobs. At sea, it was not unusual to put in a sixteen-hour day.

Also, the bow and crow's nest watches were divided into two-hour segments. The crewmen standing these watches would be on duty for four hours, but the time was divided into two two-hour-segments. The men on duty would rotate with the bridge lookouts. Looking for mines or other floating objects required intense concentration. After two hours your mind would starts to wander and your eyes tended to see things that were not there.

When I was a member of the deck force, I stood numerous bow and crow's nest watches. In heavy seas, the ship would dip into troughs in the ocean and, at times, shower like spray or the white water tip of a wave would surge over the bow.

Whenever I stood the bow watch under questionable sea conditions, I would lash myself to the bow's flagstaff to prevent a maverick wave from washing me overboard.

One time, I remember the seas were so rough that I requested permission to "secure" (or be released from standing) the bow watch. It was just too dangerous to remain at that location. The Officer of the Deck in his dry, safe enclosure on the bridge could look right down and see me standing in the washes of white seawater. It seemed like an eternity before he finally decided to grant me permission to secure the watch.

CROW'S NEST WATCH

Another dangerous lookout watch was in the crow's nests that were attached each of the two the king-post masts. One was located next to the forward hold, in front of the superstructure, and the other one was next to the aft hold, behind the superstructure of the ship. The masts supported the

USS Fergus *APA 82.*

booms, which were used to load and unload cargo from the number one and number two holds.

A steel ladder without any type of shield around it was attached to each mast. The crow's nest lookout stations were approximately fifty-feet above the ship's main deck and approximately eighty-feet above the water. To reach the protective lookout enclosures required climbing up over five stories on that exposed ladder.

Two small platforms spaced about twenty-feet apart where located on the masts. If we had difficulty or got into trouble on our way up to the crow's nest, we could step off the ladder onto one of the platforms.

Underway, we usually traveled at speeds from twelve to sixteen knots. Even in fairly calm seas, the *Fergus* had the motions of movement. Sometimes when the seas were moderate to heavy, the ship would be tilting to the extent that the crow's nest portion of the mast would be outboard from the port or starboard sides. The old timers said when you were climbing up the ladder "don't look down." If you did, and the ship was in one of its rolls, you would see boiling, white-capped seas fifty-to-eighty-feet below you. That was a white-knuckle experience.

Whenever I stood that watch and the ship was rolling in moderate to heavy seas, before going up the ladder I would secure a rope line with two loose ends around my waist. After climbing a few feet above the deck, I would reach up to shoulder height and tie a loose end of the line to a horizontal rung of the ladder. Then I would climb up to that point and repeat the procedure until I had worked my way up to the lookout station.

While on watch, we would look through binoculars for anything that could possibly endanger the ship. It was not a very desirable duty, but someone had to do it. The young seventeen, eighteen and nineteen year old deck hands in the First and Second Divisions were the "lucky ones" that were given the crow's nest assignments.

SURGERY AT SEA

As a troop transport, our secondary assignment was as a hospital ship capable of providing primary medical treatment to the combat wounded. Our ship's company included a physician; a dentist and other medical personnel trained to provide care for trauma type cases.

As a newly commissioned ship with primarily an inexperienced crew, we went through a period of intense training. We learned to work together and function as a well-organized team. Emergency duty stations drills were practiced daily in order to improve our skills and timing for any possible conditions that we might encounter.

For Dawn Alert each member of the crew went to his battle stations. At that time my GQ station was in a 40-mm gun tub as an ammunition handler. My job was to feed ammunition to the loader who put the shells into a 40-mm anti-aircraft gun that would be fired by the gun captain.

On the morning of March 15, 1945, I had been in the Navy over six months and was beginning to feel like a salty-sea-going-sailor. On this day, we were off the coast of Southern California in maneuvers with other APAs. When General Quarters was sounded at 0400 (4 a.m.) for the Dawn Alert, I woke up with a sore tenderness in my right side. After getting dressed and reporting to my Battle Station, the soreness became an intense pain. The pain was so severe that I started rolling around on the deck in the gun tub.

The gun captain and the other members of the gun crew laughed and teased me. They said, "Come on, Reding. What's the matter with you? Are you a landlubber or a sailor? The seas are calm. Wait until you get into some rough weather."

Holding my right side, I curled up in a fetal position. They thought I was seasick. The pain became so intense that I requested permission to be excused from General Quarters to report to sick bay. The telephone talker in the gun tub contacted the Combat Information Center (CIC) and said that he had a sick man in the gun tub. Permission was requested for me to be relieved from GQ and report to sick bay. The request was granted and I immediately went to the pharmacist's mate at his sickbay battle station. He took one look at me and quickly contacted the surgeon.

Lieutenant G. M. Cazan, Jr., our surgeon, was from Martins Ferry, Ohio. Dr. Cazan examined the swollen painful area on the lower, right-hand side of my abdomen. He said that I had acute appendicitis and required immediate surgery.

We were then in a heavy rolling sea, but he said that I had to have the operation "right now." The doctor assembled his surgical team and I was their first patient.

It was an apprehensive experience to be the first surgery on a new ship in a heavy rolling sea with a medical team that had been together for only a few weeks. But I was in such intense pain that I didn't really care who operated on me.

Dr. Cazan did a great job in removing the ruptured appendix. He was a skilled surgeon. He left me with just a small scar as a reminder of how fortunate I was to be on a troop transport with a physician as part of the crew.

April 22, 1945, we were at sea en route to Pearl Harbor, Hawaii. We received an emergency message from the merchant ship SS *Pequot Hill*, a tanker outbound from San Pedro, California to Ulithi, in the Caroline Islands. The *Pequot Hill* had a mess steward named Woodward A. Randolph who required immediate medical treatment. We diverted our course, located the ship and pulled to within a safe distance from it.

If this had been a US Navy ship, the captain would probably have moved up alongside the *Pequot Hill* and sent a line over so that the sick man could be transferred between the two vessels. But this was a merchant tanker loaded with fuel, and our captain was cautious. There were too many variables involved. We slowed down to almost a complete stop and Captain Snyder gave the order to launch his "gig" and have it go over to pick up the sick man. Every member of our crew was on high alert. If there was a Japanese submarine in the area, both ships were vulnerable to an attack.

The seas were calm when the LCP (gig) was launched. Once it was in the water, the winds started to pick up, which caused some small white caps and swells. I went up to the signal bridge and watched our boat slowly travel to and from the *Pequot Hill*.

Boatswain Mate Second Class William F. McGinnis, from Texas, and his crew were selected for the assignment because he was considered one of our best coxswains. In the rolling sea, McGinnis positioned his boat alongside the lee side of the merchant vessel. In his boat was a wire basket emergency stretcher for hoisting wounded or injured personnel. After the stretcher was lifted to the deck of the merchant ship, the sick man was strapped into it and the basket was then slowly lowered into the bobbing boat.

When they arrived back alongside our ship, the stretcher with the seaman in it was gently hoisted aboard. With the man safely on deck, the boat and its crew were quickly hoisted back aboard ship. The captain then immediately issued the order to resume course at flank speed of nineteen point five knots. Once we were well clear of the tanker and back on course, we slowed down to our standard speed of sixteen knots.

Dr. Cazan diagnosed the merchant seaman as having an acute case of appendicitis, which would require immediate surgery. Woodward A. Randolph, Mess Steward from the *Pequot Hill* became the second patient within one month to be operated on aboard our ship for appendicitis.

Some of the smaller ships and submarines only had pharmacist mates to turn to in the event of an emergency. I have heard stories where pharmacist mates, under emergency conditions, reviewed "the Book" and performed operations as a member of the crew read each step of the procedure to them.

SAILORS AND THEIR TATTOOS

A question often asked is, "Why do sailors get tattoos?" I am not sure. Tradition, long months at sea, and waterfront environments seem to be contributing factors. Deck-hands on the old-time sailing ships, and deck-hands on our present day warships, traditionally seem to be the sailors with tattoos.

They say the custom goes back to the old sailing days when seamen climbed the riggings in all kinds of weather conditions. Losing a sailor over the side during heavy weather was not an uncommon occurrence. The basic rule of the sea was then, and still is, "one hand for the ship and one hand for yourself." Tattoos were and still seem to be a seaman's method of self-identification and a travelogue of where he had been. A tradition among old salts, especially the ones that had pre-war China duty, was to have elaborate, decorative markings on their chest, arms or legs.

Chief Warrant Officer (Boatswain) R.S. Caro, from Los Angeles, California, was considered by many of our crew to be the most valuable man aboard ship. As a sailor's sailor, he seemed to command more respect from the enlisted men than the captain or any of the other officers. The boatswain was about 40 years old and career regular Navy. Like many of the old salts that had spent many years at sea, he had many tattoos.

The bos'n would sit on the fantail at the rear of the ship with Chief Gunner's Mate Earnest W. Edwards, talking or playing cribbage. Each one of them had more sea duty than anyone I had ever met. Chief Edwards retired from the Navy with thirty years of service before the outbreak of World War II. Most of that service was aboard ships. When the war broke out, he was recalled to active duty.

The chief was a gentle, highly respected man. He was in charge of all of the guns aboard our ship. Lieutenant J. W. Cummins, from Ben Avon, Pittsburgh, Pennsylvania was the officer responsible for the ordinance division, but Chief Edwards was the one that really ran the division. I don't know whether or not the chief had any tattoos. He was always appropriately dressed in the uniform of the day. Even in the tropics, when he sat out on the fantail talking to other senior petty officers, I never did see him take his shirt off.

Boatswain Caro was different. He made his own rules, and I never heard anyone challenge or question him. When he sat in the sun with the chief, he would frequently remove his shirt.

The bos'n was covered with tattoos. He almost looked like he belonged in a carnival. You couldn't help but glance at him (you didn't dare stare). They were on his hands, arms and chest. He probably had them on his legs too, but he always wore long trousers. The most unusual one was on his chest. From his left shoulder to his right shoulder was the image of an eagle with its wings spread. The bird's head had large, piercing eyes. Its beak was open as if it was ready to devour its meal for the day. The ferocious creature's head was located in the middle of the bos'n's upper breastbone. The talons of the eagle were located in the region of his stomach on either side of his navel. The claws of the talons were extended as if they were ready to grasp some elusive prey.

The captain was in command of the *Fergus*, but "Bos'n Caro" ran the ship. No one challenged him. Even the Captain Snyder seemed to give him a wide berth.

One of the more common tattoos that sailors in the fleet had on their forearms was an anchor with "U.S. Navy" or some other descriptive words incorporated into its design. Also, a heart with an arrow going through it was popular. On the heart would be a scroll, and inscribed in the scroll was usually the name of the sailor's wife or girlfriend, or the word "Mom."

Another common one for sailors in the Asiatic-Pacific Theater of Operations was the image of a hula girl on the forearm, outer side of the biceps, or outer side of the calves. The hula girl would be positioned on the muscle so that when it was flexed, the dancer would move her hips like she was doing the hula.

For Marines, the image of a bulldog with "U.S. Marine Corps" printed in an arch above the head of the dog was popular. Also, many of them had a dagger with a scroll or a snake over the handle and blade of the dagger. The words "Death Before Dishonor" were inscribed on the scroll.

Our ship had twin propellers, commonly known as "screws," to drive it through the water. In port, we had a large sign, which we hung over the side of the fantail. The sign said, "Danger. Twin Screws. Keep Clear." One of the sailors from our deck force returned to the ship after a liberty in Honolulu with the image of the propellers and "Danger. Twin Screws. Keep Clear." tattooed on the cheeks of his buttocks.

Another shipmate went ashore in Honolulu unmarked and came back with two tattoos on his chest. On one side was the image of a baby smiling with the word "Sweet" underneath. On the other side of his chest was a similar image, only the baby was crying and underneath was written the word "Sour."

After being at sea for several months, there was no telling what crazy things sailors would do on liberty. This was especially true when they had too much to drink.

WRITING LETTERS TO YOUR FAMILY

We were encouraged to write to our relatives and loved ones. Most of the crew was very good about writing home. Al Herrington, from Arp and later Tyler, Texas recently related to me his experience regarding letter writing. Al was a young kid when he joined the Navy, just like me, seventeen years old. He was in the First Division Deck Force and a member of a boat crew.

One day after we had been aboard ship for about six months, the captain called him to his cabin. Rarely did the captain summon lower ranked enlisted men to his cabin, unless the sailor was in big trouble.

Apprehensively, Herrington knocked on the captain's door. The captain said come in and told him to sit down at the desk. Captain Snyder looked sternly at the seated sailor and said, "Have you written to your mother lately?" Sheepishly, Herrington answered, "No sir." The captain responded "I recently received a letter from your sister saying that you had not written to your mother since you have been aboard this ship. Do you see that pen and paper? Right now, you write your mother a letter and I am going to mail it for you." With a shaking hand, Al wrote to his mother and the captain did mail the letter.

As Herrington was leaving the cabin, the captain emphasized that he wanted him to write to his mother at least once a week, and he did. Once a week, every week during the next year that he served aboard the *Fergus*, Al faithfully wrote to his Mother.

CHAPTER IV

BECOMING A SHIP'S COOK

FEBRUARY, 1945

It was a young man's war. Most of the lower-level enlisted men on the ships of the fleet were seventeen-to-nineteen years old. A twenty-one-year-old was considered an older person. The higher-ranked enlisted men were twenty-two to thirty. Anyone in his mid to late twenties or thirties was considered to be like Grandpa; only you didn't call him that.

The majority of us were born between 1917 and 1927. We grew up during the Depression. As youngsters, many of us vividly remembered days when we didn't have enough to eat. Consequently, food was a very important part of each day.

Each division or section aboard ship provided "mess-cooks" on a rotation basis to work in the galley. When my turn came to be a mess-cook, I looked forward to being able to work in the galley and eat whatever and whenever I wanted.

As a member of the deck force, we worked all day and then stood rotation watches at night. My new assignment was to help the cooks prepare the meals, and clean up afterwards. To me—with mess-cooks to help them—the cooks had one of the best jobs on the ship. It was far superior to being a sailor in the deck force.

At that time, our watch-captain in the galley was Petty Officer First Class James B. Beavers. I asked him if he could use a "cook's striker." He told me to talk to Chief Commissary Steward Reese A. Burkenbine, who was the Non-Commissioned-Officer-In-Charge (NCOIC) of Food Service.

The Chief said yes, and told me to submit an application. I immediately went to my Second Division Officer, Ensign R. D. Loutzenhiser, from Blockton, Iowa and requested permission to be transferred to food service. He approved my request.

Most Navy cooks were trained in a Navy Cooks and Bakers School, which was a ten to twelve week course. With the accelerated expansion of the fleet, there was a shortage of trained food service personnel. The needs of the fleet were greater than the schools could fulfill. Therefore, an on-the-job "cook striker" apprenticeship program was used. I was fortunate, Chief Burkenbine accepted me as a cook striker.

On February 23, 1945, I was reassigned to the "S" Division. Thus began my career aboard the *Fergus* as a ship's cook. For me, at that time, it was the best shipboard duty assignment in the Navy.

The galley had one chief as the NCOIC, two bakers with two baker's strikers, and eight cooks with four cook's strikers. They were divided into two watches, port and starboard. Each watch had twenty-four hours on duty, and twenty-four hours off duty.

We slept in the cooks and bakers compartments. Morning wake-up call for the duty cooks and bakers would be at 0400. The master-at-arms, usually a coxswain's or boatswain's mate, would come into our compartment and wake up the duty section. Sometimes he would use choice sea-going words.

Galley personnel were subject to reveille every other day unless we had GQ Dawn Alert. Then it was up every morning at 0400 (4 a.m.). On those days, instead of the master-at-arms waking us up, it was the click of the bridge microphone followed by a calm voice announcing, "Dawn Alert. General Quarters. Man your battle stations," followed by the sound of the alarm bell.

The duty cooks reported to their battle stations, then requested relief from GQ so that they could "lay down to the galley" (go to the galley) and begin preparing the morning meal.

REPORTING FOR THE MORNING SHIFT

With reveille at 0400 for the duty section of cooks and bakers or when we were secured from General Quarters, it would take about 30 minutes for us to clean up, put on our cook's duty uniforms (clean whites or blue-denim dungarees) and report to the galley. We were usually on duty by 0430. By 0500 we would be well into the process of preparing the morning meal for the crew and our passengers.

Our duty section usually consisted of four cooks; two cook strikers and four mess-cooks. When we had passengers aboard, four to six of their personnel would be assigned to help us. Then there would be up to twelve of us working in the limited space of our galley that measured approximately 30- feet-by-forty-feet (not counting the small two-man bakery). Our watch rotation (when we would start our twenty-four-hours of being on duty) commenced at 1200 (noon) every other day.

The duty cook in charge was called the captain of the watch or watch-captain. One of the first things the he would do was to check the menus for the day and to assign the task for a cook and some mess-cooks to gather the ingredients for the meals to be prepared during our shift.

Also, he would assign one or two of our duty section the night shift to prepare and serve midnight snacks of coffee and sandwiches to personnel standing the late-night and early-morning watches. Whoever received that duty did not have to help clean-up after supper or get up early to help prepare breakfast.

The shift we were replacing would have the noon meal (dinner) prepared. We would serve the noon meal to the crew and passengers, and clean up the galley. Then we would start to prepare the evening meal (supper). After supper we would give the galley a thorough cleaning before 2000 (8 p.m.) when we secured the watch for the day.

PREPARING THE MEALS

We prepared and served up to 3,000 meals per day to the enlisted personnel of our crew and our passengers. The meals were divided into approximately 1,000 each for breakfast, dinner and supper. Civilians would call them breakfast, lunch and dinner.

The cooks and mess-cooks would be assigned the task of gathering the ingredients for the meals from the storerooms, or from one of our eight walk-in refrigerators, which were referred to as "reefers." Considering that we could be at sea for several weeks-to-months before our supplies were replenished, our refrigeration space was really limited.

The longer we were at sea, the more limited our menu choices became. After a few weeks, we began to run out of fresh, perishable produce and dairy items. Then our only dairy products were canned or powdered milk and sometimes the butter would be rancid.

Most of the meats were frozen or canned. The onions and potatoes

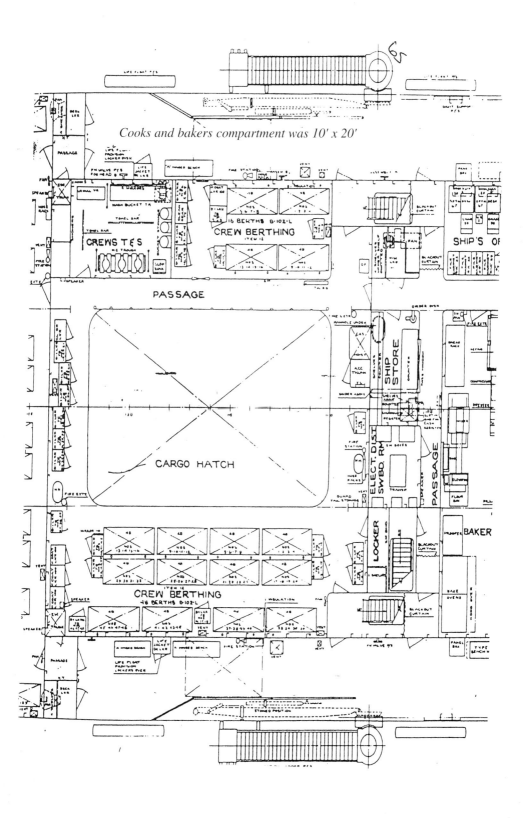

Cooks and bakers compartment was 10' x 20'

would be dehydrated and the eggs would be powdered. Most of the vegetables, such as corn, tomatoes, and peas would be canned. Almost all fruits were canned.

The cooks worked hard to keep the crew and the passengers well fed and to make sure that no one became sick from tainted food. Our firm policy regarding the safety of the food for consumption was "if in doubt, throw out."

After several months in the heat of the tropics, weevils frequently would be found in the flour, and worms would occasionally be living off the nuts in the candy bars. The crew and the troops would joke that slices of our bread were the best "single-sliced meat sandwiches" they had ever received. Thank goodness they were young and good-natured. Quantity we had. Quality—well, we tried to do our best.

Food poisoning for a crew at sea could be devastating. We took pride in serving the best chow available and having what we considered the cleanest galley in the fleet.

During the period that I was a cook aboard the *Fergus*, I cannot remember one case of anyone becoming ill from tainted food. We were proud of our high standards in our preparation and service of hearty, tasty meals.

Good-natured groans and moans were not uncommon. Overall, considering the challenging and many times adverse conditions we operated under, there were minimal complaints. Everyone knew that we were trying to do our best.

SERVING THE MEALS

The food was served cafeteria style. Separating the galley from the mess hall was a long, compartmentalized, stainless steel steam table with openings in the metal top. Hot or warm food items in stainless steel containers were put into the openings in the table. Mess-cooks stood behind the food containers and served the crew and passengers as they walked down the chow line. The plates were compartmentalized mess trays. Beverages were in metal cups.

Our mess hall tables were made of metal with green poured linoleum tops that had metal lips around the top sides. The linoleum tops helped prevent the metal trays from sliding around; the metal lips kept food trays and beverage cups from falling off the table during rough weather.

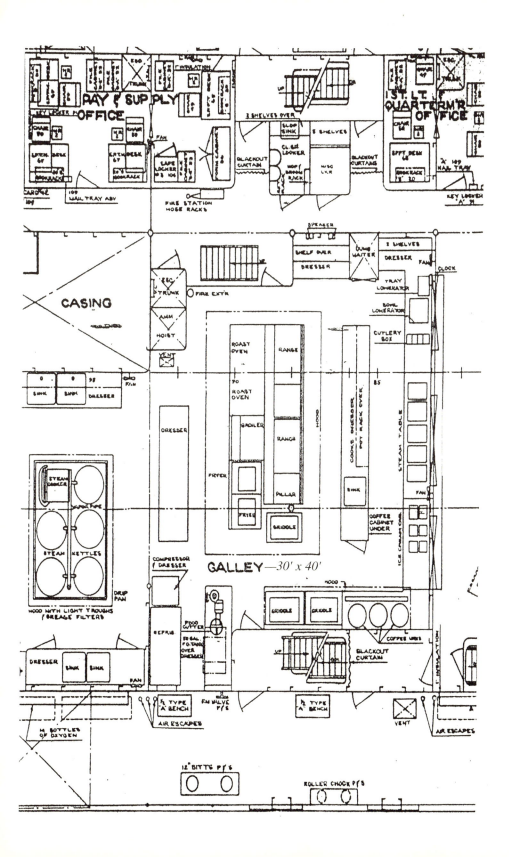

Whenever we had troops aboard the mess hall was very crowded. In order to help move the men along so that they quickly ate their meals and didn't linger in the limited space of the eating area, we put extension legs on the mess tables. The extended legs raised the tables up to waist height so that the men ate their meals in a standing position. This greatly reduced the lingering mealtime socializing, thereby creating a quicker table-space turn over.

If they didn't have anything scheduled that day, sometimes the troops would line up in the passageways an hour or two before we started serving meals. When they finished eating, they would go up on deck for a while or back to their quarters. After an hour or so, they would simply go back in line to wait for the next meal. You would see them reading books, writing letters, talking or just standing there with bored looks of resignation on their faces.

In heavy seas, many times it was difficult to walk down the passageways without holding onto the bulkheads (walls). To climb a ladder from one deck level to the next sometimes could be a real challenge. We were a cargo-carrying troop ship with a comparatively shallow draft. Therefore, even under what we would consider normal sea conditions, the *Fergus* would respond more to the tossing, rolling movements of the seas than other ships with more powerful engines and deeper, more streamlined hulls.

In rough weather, as you tried to eat while standing, you would brace yourself against the table or the bulkhead. At the same time, you would hold onto the mess tray with one hand to steady it. With the other hand you had the adventure of trying to pick up the food with a fork, and get the food into your mouth without stabbing yourself. Trying to drink coffee under those conditions was a feat in itself.

If you have ever attempted to eat or drink during a rough weather ride in an airplane, then you have an idea of what it is like to try to eat aboard ship in heavy weather. Then compound it by trying to eat while standing up. The mess lines were usually short when we were in heavy seas. Most of the troops would eat only one or two meals a day. They would rather ride out the weather by staying in their bunks.

When we didn't have troops aboard the ship, the mess tables were returned to their normal level so that the crew could sit down for their meals, or use the mess facilities to read, write letters or talk. Also, during

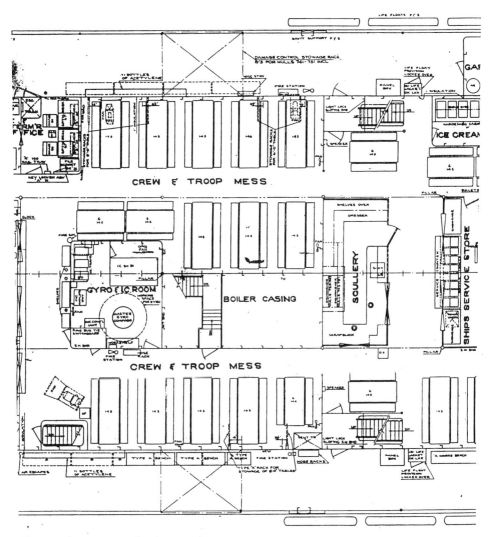

Crew and troop mess (eating area).

inclement weather, movies—if they were available—were shown in the mess hall.

The job of a cook was demanding, but it was much better than standing deck or lookout watches. Best of all, cooks never had to wait in chow lines.

BREAKFAST, DINNER AND SUPPER

The menus from the Cook Book of the United States Navy, 1944 edition, called for meals that provided the men with 3,000 to 4,500 calories per day.

Sample menus were provided for spring, summer, fall and winter. We were in the tropics most of the time; therefore our recommended meals were frequently modified to fit the availability of canned, frozen or local foods.

The mealtime selections would vary depending upon whether we had troops aboard or not. Without troops, we could feed the crew a more personalized breakfast such as fried eggs, if we had fresh eggs available. With troops aboard, whether the eggs were fresh or powdered, they were always scrambled.

We didn't have the time, space or personnel to serve almost a thousand men custom meals. The powdered eggs, if seasoned properly, tasted pretty good. Chow was an assembly-line type of operation. A sample breakfast would be:

Chilled fresh plums or canned stewed prunes
Dry Cereals with fresh or powdered milk
Scrambled eggs
Crisp bacon
Sugar donuts (fresh that morning)
Toast with butter
Coffee and milk

The recipe for Scrambled Eggs to serve 1,000 men would be:

2400 fresh eggs (thirty gallons)
60 tablespoons of salt
7-1/2 tablespoons of pepper
30 gallons of milk (powered or fresh)
20 pounds of melted butter or other fat

The eggs, salt, pepper and milk were combined into large mixing bowls and thoroughly blended with an electric beater. When fresh eggs and milk were not available, powdered eggs and milk would be used. If the stainless-steel fry top of the range or the stainless-steel frying pans were used, you would heat some fat—usually bacon fat—and add the egg mixture. Constant stirring was required to slowly heat the mixture until it reached the proper consistency. When the large steam-heated kettle was used, the same basic "add and stir" technique would be followed. On an as needed basis, thirty gallons of scrambled eggs would be put into stainless steel containers and placed into slots in the steam-table serving line.

Good judgment and timing were very important to ensure that the ingredients were properly prepared, and that the meal was ready when the mess call was sounded over the ship's public address system.

One or two of the following food items would also be served with the eggs. Included was a new canned meat product—Spam—that was a combination of ham and "other ingredients."

Diced ham (or spam): 102 pounds
Diced bacon: 120 pounds
Luncheon meat: 120 pounds
Pork sausage: 160 pounds
American cheese: 80 pounds

The mess-cooks, under the supervision of a duty-cook, drew the monotonous tasks of cracking eggs, or peeling carrots, potatoes and onions. Up to two hundred dozen (2,400) eggs would be used for breakfast. Two of the mess-cooks would sit with a crate of eggs between their legs. They would take one egg in each hand, crack them and drop the contents into large metal container and the shells into a cardboard box. Usually it would take them several minutes to develop a rhythm of coordinating both hands in order to pick up the eggs and simultaneously crack them. During that learning process, usually a few pieces of eggshells would fall into the containers. Most of the particles would be removed, but the fragments of shells that were left became another ingredient in the scrambled eggs.

At the same time, another pair would be peeling onions. We tried to put the onions into water so that we didn't have teary-eyed mess-cooks.

To peel potatoes, a large electric powered container was used. On the inside of the container's drum was an abrasive sandpaper-type coating. The potatoes would be washed and placed into the peeler, which when turned on would toss them around against the abrasive sides. This process removed most of the skin. Once peeled, they would require that the dark spots or "eyes" be removed. This was called "eyeing the potato," and the mess-cooks did it by hand, one at a time. The menu of the day would determine if the potatoes would be sliced, sectioned, diced, boiled or baked.

At the same time, other members of the watch crew would be at the grill preparing the main course items on the menu.

The American sailor's shipboard beverage of choice was coffee. The crew and the passengers commonly referred to it as mud or joe. One of the first things that we did when we reported to the galley for our morning shift was "freshen the pot." That meant we made a large, fresh container of coffee. Rarely did we serve tea. We tried to keep the pot of "joe" full, brewing and available for the crew and passengers twenty-four hours a day.

After the war was over, things were more relaxed. When we were in port and whenever members of the crew returned from liberty late at night, most of them just wanted a cup of joe and if available, a bite to eat. Once aboard ship, usually their first stop was the mess hall.

We were not required to feed returning liberty parties. It was extra work for the duty cooks to fix late-night snacks, but we did to help out our shipmates.

On the late night shift as duty-cook, we used the concept that tips were the oil that made the wheels of progress turn quickly and smoothly. We placed a large, empty pickle jar on the serving counter that separated the galley from the crew's mess (eating area). Taped to the empty jar was a large cartoon sketch of a cat with a sign saying, "Feed the kitty and the kitty will feed you." The kitty jar was against Navy rules and regulations, but the crew didn't seem to mind, and no one ever said anything.

Most of the time the returning enlisted crewmembers had been drinking and they were hungry. They would throw some of their extra change into the kitty jar, which would give us a few extra dollars when we went ashore on liberty.

MORNING CHOW

Breakfast would be prepared between 0430 (4:30 a.m.) and 0600 (6:00 a.m.). At 0545 "mess gear," which was better known as "chow down," would be announced (piped) over the ship's Public Address system to notify the ship's company and the passengers that breakfast would start being served at 0600.

When we had troops aboard, almost an hour before the announcement, they would be forming a chow line in the passageway adjacent to the entrance to the mess hall. Members of the crew's ship's company—because they had to go to work or stand watches—were allowed to go to the front of the line.

The breakfast that drew the most moans, but was actually liked by the crew and passengers had many unofficial names. One of them had the initials "SOS." The meal consisted of:

Fresh or canned fruit

SOS (creamed chipped beef or hamburger on cornbread or toast)

Pastry

Jam

Coffee and milk

Another "groaning" favorite was:

Fresh or canned fruit

Hot cereal

Navy baked beans with salt pork

Danish twist or other type pastry

Coffee and milk

The most popular breakfast pastry was cinnamon and raisin rolls with lots of vanilla icing.

DINNER

(Civilians would call this meal lunch.)

Roast lamb with mint jelly

Scalloped potatoes

Buttered asparagus (or other vegetable)

Apple, carrot and celery salad

Chilled fresh or canned fruit

Hot biscuits with butter

Ice tea

Another favorite meal was:

Green split pea (or other vegetable) soup

Roast beef with natural gravy

Lyonnaise potatoes

Harvard beets

Carrot and celery salad
Ice cream
Hot rolls with butter
Coffee and milk

SUPPER
(Civilians would call this meal dinner.)
Baked pork chops or grilled Salisbury steak
Potatoes au gratin
Buttered green beans
Mixed vegetable salad
Pineapple upside-down cake
Fresh baked bread with butter
Coffee, milk or fruit-ade

For special days such as Thanksgiving, Christmas and Easter, considering the food items and ingredients we had available, we would prepare the meal as close to the traditional holiday menus as we possibly could.

DESSERTS

Most of the cooks and bakers were Navy trained. Occasionally a cook or a baker would be a professional from civilian life. Then you had a treat.

We were fortunate to have a very talented civilian-trained baker aboard our ship. He was Baker Second Class Charles R. Eggenbrecth, from Allendale, Illinois. Eggenbrecth had the touch of a gourmet pastry chef. The crew's favorite was his pineapple upside-down cake, which he would create on large sheet cake pans in sufficient quantity to feed 1,500 men.

He didn't always use the Navy's cookbook. For many of the recipes he would add additional ingredients, which he kept to himself. His pineapple upside-down cake was the best I have ever tasted. I think his secret was to blend the right amount of crushed pineapple along with its juice into the cake batter.

Over fifty years later, at one of the ship's reunions, some of the crew's fondest memories aboard the *Fergus* were the early morning odors of fresh baking bread, the brewing coffee, the pastries and especially Eggenbrecth's pineapple upside-down cakes.

THANKSGIVING DINNER AT SEA

On Thanksgiving Day in November 1945, we were in the Western Pacific en route from Guam, Mariana Islands to Tacloban in the Philippine Islands. We had been at sea almost continually for the better part of a year.

Whenever we pulled into port, we would stay one or two days—just long enough to unload our troops and cargo, replenish our basic supplies and take on new passengers and cargo—before we got underway.

Thanksgiving dinner was served at noon. Many of our staple food items had been in our ship's storerooms in the tropical heat for over ten months.

THE MENU:
Chilled tomato juice (The boxes had been damaged and the contents
                were questionable, so we didn't serve the tomato juice)
Roasted turkey (frozen young tom turkey)
Virginia baked ham (canned)
Bread dressing (The flour for the bread dressing had weevils in it)
Giblet gravy
Mashed sweet potatoes (dehydrated)
Cranberry sauce (dehydrated)
Buttered corn (canned)
Celery stalks (mildewed)
Mincemeat pie
Hot rolls
Ice cream (We didn't have the ingredients on the ship to make
                ice cream, so we served chocolate cake instead)
Cigars (stale from the humidity)
Cigarettes (also stale)
Candy (some of the chocolate bars with peanuts had worms)
Mixed nuts (more worms in the nuts)
Iced tea or coffee

We received many smiles and good-natured comments about the

weevils, worms and staleness. We didn't hear any real complaints.

Considering the time, place and conditions, every meal was as appetizing as we could possibly make it. The key ingredients to take the blandness out of monotonous food items were "S&S" (salt and sugar) plus—whenever possible—ample use of butter.

When we had a full complement of troops aboard, our facilities were stretched to the maximum. The galley was busy almost twenty-four hours a day.

The fresh water on our ship was constantly being monitored for impurities. Most of the water we used for drinking and cooking purposes came from our ship's evaporators. In port—when available—a Navy barge would pull up alongside to replenished our supply of the fresh drinkable water.

In the Philippines we had a problem. We had picked up some bad water from a Navy barge. The water was piped from our holding tanks into the ship's drinking-fountain system. It made some of the crew, and quite a few passengers, sick with diarrhea. In the galley as an additional safeguard to insure the safety of the water we used in the cooking and cleaning process, we tried to heat it to a sufficient temperature to destroy any impurities.

When Chief Reese A. Burkenbine was transferred off the ship, our senior ranking petty officer, Ship's Cook First Class Jim Beavers, was promoted to be the Chief Commissary Steward. He was then the petty officer in charge of the ship's food service program. Chief Beavers, like Chief Burkenbine, was a professional. He was very patient—almost like a schoolteacher—in the way he helped us.

He encouraged us to have pride in the food we served. He helped us to expand our knowledge of the art of cooking, and continually emphasized that cleanliness was essential in the preparation and serving of meals.

LOADING AMMUNITION

As cooks we had twenty-four hours on duty and twenty-four hours off. During our twenty-four hours off—depending on the requirements of the ship—cooks were free from any work detail except during times of "maximum effort." Then we did whatever was needed to help. We loaded cargo, did relief deck work, stood lookout watches and any other duty assignments necessary. Some of the jobs were loading supplies, including live ammunition.

Loading ammo for our ship's guns and our passengers' weapons was dangerous work. Members of our crew would form loading lines. Boxes of ammunition including mortar shells and hand grenades would be passed, by hand, from one crewmember to the next.

We heard that in the May of 1944, at Pearl Harbor—during such a loading process—six Landing Ship Tanks (LSTs) blew up. The explosions resulted in a considerable loss of lives among the crew and naval personnel in the loading area.

Also, in July of 1944, at Port Chicago, on the other side of the bay from San Francisco, California, two freighters that were being loaded with explosives blew up, killing and wounding a large number of the Navy ammunition handlers and merchant seaman. Working around such volatile cargo was a "no mistake job."

CHAPTER V

TROOPS ABOARD SHIP

FIRST FEW DAYS AT SEA

With troops aboard, several hundred of them would be assigned to each of the four open bays in our cargo holds. Up to 336 troops could be consigned to one bay. These crowded quarters were more confining and considerably less comfortable than the crew's living quarters. The crew bunks were stacked three-to-four tiers high. Troop bunks were four tiers high. The troop toilet facilities were in large open rooms with zero privacy. Their communal showers were usually salt water. If we had a surplus of fresh water, then occasionally it would be available to them for showering.

Most of these men were from Middle America. The largest body of water many of them had ever seen was a large river or lake. The mental and emotional discipline demanded of 600 to 700 men confined in cramped, claustrophobic quarters for prolonged periods of time, aboard a ship at sea, was a demanding challenge.

The hazardous conditions of wartime travel; with the potential of being attacked by enemy submarines or struck by a loose floating mine was a stressful experience. In an attempt to make their time aboard our ship as comfortable and as endurable as possible—considering the wartime circumstances—we provided our passengers with nutritious meals. But sometimes food was used for other purposes.

Whenever we had new passengers aboard the *Fergus*, the first meal we served them after we were underway ——was greasy pork chops. This was done on purpose. The greasy pork chops, combined with the rocking and rolling motion of the ship, made quite a few of them seasick. Being

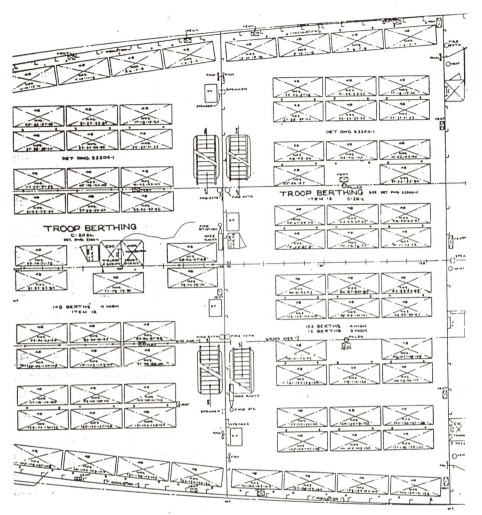

Troop berthing over #2 hold had 336 bunks which were stacked four tiers high. #1 hold in the forward part of the ship had similar accommodations for the troops.

seasick actually calmed them down, took their minds off of their crowded living conditions, and helped them to forget why they were aboard our ship and where they were going.

One of the initial announcements that the troops heard when they were getting settled in their quarters was, "If you should have an upset stomach, feel uncomfortable, or get light headed, go topside and stand on the lee side of the deck. Don't have the wind blow into your face."

Once we were underway, our personnel would be standing by with saltwater hoses to wash down the decks, and to help to clean up any soldier that made the mistake of going to the windward side of the ship.

It was amazing how the motion of the sea, combined with the greasy pork chops, had a calming effect on any apprehension, which the troops might have had. If we did that today, there would probably be a congressional investigation into our cruel "greasy pork chops anxiety therapy." But it worked. After a few days at sea, usually our passengers settled into a shipboard routine and were molded into workable groups.

DEVELOPING A SHIPBOARD ROUTINE

Within a week, almost all of the troops began to think like sailors. They soon learned to respond to orders issued over the ship's PA system. Most of those commands were preceded by the sound of the boatswain's pipe and the words "Now Hear This."

During emergencies, things happened quickly. When an alarm was sounded, the troops were ordered to move out of the passageway traffic-flow pattern and freeze in position. They were to remain there until the ship's company was at their emergency stations.

The troops would then be given instructions over the ship's PA system. If the PA system failed, directions would be given by word of mouth for them to go to their assigned assembly points.

Aboard United States naval vessels, there was a standard traffic-flow pattern, which all hands followed—especially during emergencies. The traffic-flow pattern was "Starboard Up and Forward; Port, Down and Aft." This meant: when facing the bow (or front)—if you are on the left-hand (port) side of the ship, the traffic flow is down the ladders and to the rear of the ship. If you are on the right-hand (starboard) side of the ship, the traffic flow is up the ladders and forward.

There were markings on the bulkheads (walls) to indicate where you were located on the ship. The *Fergus* was not a very wide vessel (fifty-eight feet), so when the alarms sounded, men could quickly move across to either the port or starboard side as needed.

Our Marines were basically in charge of the troops. Their officers, with the approval of our Marine Detachment Commander, organized their daily training and recreation schedules. If any discipline or incarceration were required, our Marines would take care of the problem.

On the *Fergus*, we had two cargo storage areas called hatches. The hatch openings were covered with several sections of large, rectangular steel designed to fit together with overlapping edges. These hatch covers formed a metal roof over the holds of the ship. On top of the hatch covers, large, heavy canvas tarpaulins were placed to form a watertight seal.

The canvas-covered number two hatches served as the ship's outdoor stage or arena. During the daylight hours the area was used for musical entertainment, or as a boxing arena for amateur matches. On our first trip out, we had marine passengers aboard. Several of them had musical instruments and they formed a band. It was great to hear live music. They were really good.

At night, if blackout regulations were not in effect, a canvas screen would be hung between the two booms attached to the aft mast. The area would then become our outdoor movie theater. Briefings for the troops by their platoon or squad leaders would be held in the passenger quarters, or almost anywhere topside in non-crew work areas.

When the troops had any free time during the long days at sea, they filled the hours by standing in chow lines, sitting topside in the tropical sun, writing letters home, playing cards or just laying on their bunks.

Card playing was one of their favorite activities, even though there were signs against it posted in the troop-berthing quarters and at other common gathering points. The notices said, "Gambling is strictly forbidden aboard this vessel." They were signed by one of our officers, Ensign M. S. Peterman from Monroe, Michigan. Poor Mr. Peterman—he had the frustrating task of trying to enforce the no gambling rule.

Aboard ship, the junior grade officers were usually given the undesirable (to almost impossible) assignments of trying to alter or control the habits of the enlisted personnel. At times there would be more money changing hands at a card game in one of our troop compartments than at the card tables in a small-time gambling casino in Reno, Nevada.

Under wartime conditions, we darkened ship at night. From sundown until sunrise—even though the seas might be calm and the tropical nights might be beautiful and pleasant—for security reasons, only authorized ship's company personnel were allowed on deck.

The passengers and off-duty members of the crew were restricted to the interior of the ship. They were requested to stay in close proximity to their quarters where unfortunately the air was usually hot, humid, and stale.

During the war, the closer we came to the combat zones, the troops—on their own—used their leisure time cleaning their weapons, sharpening their knives and bayonets, and just generally checking their equipment. Mentally and physically there was a change. You could see the increase in their alertness as they prepared themselves and their equipment for combat.

"SHAKE DOWN CRUISE"

After the *Fergus* was first commissioned, we took it out what is called a "shakedown cruise," where we did trial runs and conducted exercises to determine if the ship and the crew were ready to go to war. One of the first things we conducted was emergency drills. Daily we practiced to improve our speed and efficiency.

The quickness, which our crew responded to an emergency, could give us the edge for survival-this especially applied to our General Quarters battle stations. At the beginning of the "shake down" cruise we were slow. It took over fifteen minutes for all hands to have our battle stations "manned and ready."

After several weeks of daily practice, our battle stations were manned and ready within five minutes after the alarm was sounded. A few months later, when we were in the war zone, the time was further reduced to three minutes or less—depending on the time of the day or night and whether we were sailing in, smooth, heavy or stormy seas. We became a well-trained, highly disciplined crew. We thought we were the best in the Navy.

Ships are divided into sections, or compartments, which can be made watertight. When a ship is hit or damaged—if all of the doors and hatchways are properly secured—there will hopefully be sufficient buoyancy to keep the vessel afloat.

When we had troops aboard, they were instructed to have their life belts in their possession at all times. If we ever had to abandon ship, they wouldn't have the time to look for lifesaving devices.

The life preserver belt was approximately four inches wide, and made from a rubber-like material. At one end of the belt were two small CO_2 cartridges that—when squeezed—would puncture the end of the cylinders and released the gas which would inflate the life belt.

If Abandon Ship was ordered, we were instructed to, if possible, go to our abandon ship stations and leave the vessel in an orderly manner. If we had to go into the water, we should try to locate, swim to and climb aboard a life raft or one of our boats. On our ship, we carried life rafts in addition to our LCVP boats and one LCP boat. In an emergency, if we had the time to launch all of the boats and rafts, we would have more than sufficient life-saving capacity for all of our passengers and crew.

The life rafts could quickly be cut loose and dropped into the water. Each of the gray oval flotation devices contained food, water kegs, flares, fishing gear and other items for survival for at sea for a prolonged period of time. The boats—if we had time and were able to launch them—also carried survival gear.

Some of my shipmates had been on vessels that were sunk in combat. They said that things happened very fast. Your training coupled with luck and your instincts took over. Considering everything, if we had to abandon ship, our best chance for initial survival was our life vest or life jacket that we were suppose to have with us at all times.

TURK'S HEAD

Ships of the fleet were frequently decorated with intricate knots made with white twine. There was a sense of competitive pride in the way that your ship looked, especially the bridge and the in-port-quarterdeck. On the long voyages across the oceans of the world, as a way to give their drab looking vessels a sense of individuality, members of the deck force would weave interesting designs around many of the oval-shaped pipes or handles on the ship.

One of the more popular and difficult knots to weave is the "Turk's Head." A good Turk's head took patience and manual dexterity to create. Aboard the *Fergus*, some of our boatswain's mates were highly skilled at making such knots.

One of those was Jimmie Golden, from Texas. He was the coxswain of the captain's gig. Golden did an impressive job of decorating the "gig" with numerous intricate knots. Whenever we pulled into port, our captain's gig was one of the sharpest-looking boats in the water.

Aboard ship, most of us wore or carried knives for emergency purposes such as cutting a line or if we had to abandon ship to hopefully help protect us from sharks or other predators of the sea. I wore a hunting knife in a sheath on my uniform belt. The ship's machinist helped me to shape and sharpen the blade so that it had cutting edges on both sides. I still have my knife. On the upper portion of the handle is a "Turk's Head" knot which a boatswain mate showed me how to weave. For an amateur, it looks good.

TO THE WAR ZONE

On April 19, 1945, at San Diego, California, we took aboard 682 Marines—including 15 officers and 526 enlisted men—from the 57th Replacement Draft, Casual Battalion, Camp Joseph H. Pendleton. This would be our first voyage to the war zone.

Our passengers were combat-ready Marines. They were battlefield replacements. In other words, they would replace men in combat units that had been either killed or wounded. Our job was to take them across the Pacific Ocean and land them on hostile shores. After the war was over, I learned that almost one hundred percent of those young Marines became casualties (killed or wounded) during the final stages of the battle for Okinawa.

Our section had liberty the day before we sailed. Several of us went ashore together. We were supposed to be back aboard ship by 10 p.m. In San Diego they had what were called "Dime-A-Dance Halls." They were usually in a building that had a bar with a large dance floor. Girls in their twenties were employed, on a commission basis, to dance with customers. Each dance would cost ten cents. A customer could buy several tickets and ask one of the girls that sat around the perimeter of the dance floor to dance. The place was patrolled and controlled by bouncers.

Most of the sailors wanted female companionship. They just wanted to talk and if possible dance with a girl. As a customer, if you were over twenty-one, you could buy a drink. If weren't twenty-one, you would have a shipmate buy a drink for you. We arrived at the dance hall in the early evening. After a few drinks, a sailor from the *Fergus* got into an argument with a sailor from another ship. A fight started. We went over to help our shipmate.

The bouncers came over to break it up, and the Shore Patrol was called. About the time we were starting to help our shipmates, the SPs showed up at the door. Three of us were picked up by the Shore Patrol and transported to the San Diego Navy Brig which was adjacent to fleet landing. The other sailors got away and went back to the ship.

Being picked up by the SP's was a sobering experience. We had troops aboard, and we knew that we were about ready to get underway heading westward. Missing ship would have meant a General Court Martial and possible prison time. We explained to them what the situation was, but they would not release us to go back to the ship. They held us overnight in a stark cold cell.

Early the next morning, the guards at the brig woke us up and marched the three of us to a liberty launch at the nearby fleet landing. Under the supervision of an armed escort, we were returned to our ship. Upon arrival back aboard the *Fergus*, we were told to go to our duty stations. Soon afterwards, the "special sea detail" was set and we got underway.

We didn't know what was going to happen to us. After several days at sea we expected to have a Captain's or Executive Officer's Mast and be punished. But nothing happened; no one said a word to us about the entire incident.

Later, I learned that in the confusion of sailing westward with combat Marines aboard, one of our yeomen conveniently lost the paperwork regarding our "overnight stay" in the San Diego Brig. Nothing was ever said about it, and no indication was made on our records, other than a notation in the Ship's Log that that we had been returned to the ship under armed guard by the local Shore Patrol.

From San Diego, we sailed to Pearl Harbor on the island of Oahu in the Hawaiian Islands. After seeing some of the old movies, like Mutiny on the Bounty and other South Sea Island films, I visualized small villages along beautiful tropical beaches with grass shacks and native girls running around in hula skirts. My imagination had really run wild. Boy, was I in for a disappointment.

When we sighted the island of Oahu, I went up to the signal bridge and looked through the signalmen's powerful binoculars hoping to see grass shacks and hula girls. All I saw were concrete and stucco buildings, Navy ships and white-hatted sailors. Welcome to the tropical paradise of Oahu.

At Pearl Harbor no one received liberty. We were in port just long enough to take on fuel, supplies and some special cargo. We then traveled to the eastern side of the island of Maui, which is near Oahu. At Maui, our ship's crew and our troops participated in practicing amphibious landings under simulated combat conditions. No one received liberty. The only ones that got ashore were the troops and the boat crews.

After four days of intense training, we were honed to be mentally and physically ready for combat. From Maui, we headed southwest.

With troops aboard, the ship was very congested. The crew worked long hours under stressful conditions. If we had any free time, we usually tried to catch up on our lost sleep. Under such crowded conditions there wasn't much space available where you could be by yourself. Still, we each seemed to locate special place to be alone in the crowd. My favorite spot was on the fantail.

For the troops it was more difficult for them to mentally get away from the pressure of their highly restricted living conditions. Their quarters were crowded and smelled of men, gear and equipment. To give them some sort of relief, they were allowed on deck on a rotation basis for exercise, and fresh air. After a few days in the tropical seas, everyone seemed to become more irritable and edgier than usual. Tempers flared and we had some fights on deck and in the troop-berthing areas.

To help ease the strain of the monotony and pressure of going to battle, the officers and non-commissioned officers planned daily drills, physical-fitness exercises and recreational activities to keep all the personnel busy and focused.

Aboard ship we had a piano and a set of drums. Some of the Marines brought their musical instruments such as guitars, trumpets and harmonicas with them. Under the tropical sun, we had the pleasure of watching several first class musical variety shows on an improvised stage on the aft hold. Some of the marine musicians and entertainers were really talented. It was a treat.

We also had some boxing matches. Crewmembers or representatives from different marine squads could challenge each other. The bouts were held according to weight divisions. With the enthusiasm generated, you would think each fight was a contest for the world's championship.

The passengers had a vocabulary of their own. They called their second lieutenants "shave tails." I asked one of the old sergeants why. He told me that the origin of the term "shave tail" goes back to the days when horses and mules were the primary mode of moving men and equipment. Whenever a new mule was brought into the pack, its tail was shaved so that the muleskinners could watch out for it until they had it trained to work with the rest of the pack.

Therefore, the term shave tail was attached to newly commissioned second lieutenants. They bore the designation until the sergeants and the experienced enlisted men had trained the new officers to fit in with the way things were done in the real military. Another phrase that they used was "by shank's mare," which meant to walk or march.

The further we traveled southwest across the Pacific Ocean, the greater were the hazards from floating mines or enemy submarines. As we were approaching the International Dateline (180 degrees longitude), they announced over the public address system that we could expect an attack from the enemy at any time of the day or night.

INTERNATIONAL DATELINE

In the late 1870s, Sanford Fleming, a Canadian railway planner-engineer outlined a plan for worldwide time zones. In the year 1884 delegates from 27 nations met in Washington, DC and agreed upon a system based upon Fleming's concept.

A circle has 360 degrees. The world was divided into a grid pattern of horizontal and vertical lines separated by degrees. The divisions on the grid pattern were called lines of longitude and latitude.

Fleming's system is designed around having 24 standard lines of Longitude called meridians that run from the North Pole to the South Pole, at right angles to the Equator. These meridians are 15 degrees apart starting with zero degrees that located at Greenwich, England and known as the Prime Meridian. Civilians refer to this zero degrees Longitude as Greenwich Means Time (GMT). The military and airlines refer to it as Zulu (Z) time.

The 180th-degree line of longitude is known as the International Dateline. Traveling westward, when you cross the International Dateline, you gain one day (a Monday becomes a Tuesday). Going eastward, you lose a day (a Monday becomes a Sunday).

Crossing the Equator or the International Dateline aboard a ship meant that you had spent weeks and even months at sea. To break the monotony of the shipboard routine, rites of passage were established to initiate those about to "Cross the Line" and enter "Neptune's Kingdom" for the first time. Once they were properly initiated, they would forever be known as "Shellbacks." Prior to the initiation the pathetic creatures from the lands across the seas were referred to as "Pollywogs."

Whenever a ship "Crossed the Line" it was the "Shellbacks" sacred duty and responsibility to make sure that all of the "Pollywogs" aboard the vessel were properly initiated and fully qualified to enter in the world of King Neptune. The supreme ruler of the seas of the world was known as "King Rex."

To soften the increasing shipboard tension and to help us temporarily take our minds off of what lay ahead, the captain decided that the Pollywogs aboard the *Fergus* would be initiated into the "Sacred Order of the Golden Dragon."

As supreme ruler of his watery domain, King Rex, on May 13, 1945, issued the following orders to the passengers and crew of the USS *Fergus* (APA 82):

HEAR YE, HEAR YE, THIS IS THE DAY

A message has been received direct from the Mandarin via the Ocean Waves, as follows: "Greetings fellow Dragons of the Golden Society. In checking my records, I find you are due in my Domain today. In your midst, I find clinging barnacles, slimy seaweed, pollywogs and those who brave entrance to my darkened depth that surround you. Prepare them all for Dragon Meat, for today My Royal Court and I will board your ship to purge those hands about to enter my Kingdom.

—By the Order of King Rex

The Royal Court consisted of members of the crew and passengers who had previously been initiated into the rites of the Golden Dragon. After the names of the members of the royal court were the letters USN (United States Navy) or USMC (United States Marine Corps). This meant that these men were career or "regular" military, not "reservist" (USNR and USMCR) like most of us.

They were the backbone of the Fleet and the Corp. They were the ones that had caught the brunt of the carnage of the first delicate months of the conflict. As regulars, they had been in the war zone before.

Their stability, strength and experience were a major reason why our country had been able to hold the enemy at bay while we were able to build up our armed forces. They were the ones that helped to transform inexperienced recruits into sailors to man the rapidly expanding ships of the fleet and Marines to land on hostile shores.

! HEAR YE, HEAR YE, THIS IS THE DAY! .

A message has been received direct from the Mandarin Via the Ocean Waves, as follows: "Greetings fellow Dragons of the Golden Society, in checking my records I find you are Due in my domain today and in your midst I find you surrounded by clinging barnacles, slimy seaweed, polly-wogs and those who brav entrance to my darkened depth. Prepair them all for Dragons Meat, for today my Royal court and I will board to purge those hands who wish to cross."

"Alfred wants to know if he couldn't wait and be iniated the Next time we cross the line"

By

Nuf Sed

"Who's a Golden DRAGON"!?

Yota Thee I ben thick

THE ROYAL COURT IS :

ROYAL MANDARIN:
  Chief Commissary Steward England, USN
ROYAL MANDARIN'S DAUGHTER:
  Boatswains Mate 2nd/c McGinnis, USN
ROYAL BABY:
  1st Sgt. Dean, USMC
ROYAL PRINCESS:
  Pvt. Tilman, USMC—How did a private in the United States
                    Marine Corps ever become a member of
                    such an elite, high-ranking court?
ROYAL JUSTICE:
  Chief Motor Machinist's Mate Lauth, USN
ROYAL LAW GIVERS:
  Gunner's Mate 2/c "Blackie" Allegri, USN
  1st Sgt. Lecount, USMC
ROYAL ARTIST: 1st Sgt. MacHale, USMC
ROYAL PHOTOGRAPHERS:
  Lt. Cazan, USN
  Lt. McManus, USN
ROYAL SANITATION CREW:
  Coxswain Franxman, USN
  Boatswain Mate 1st/c Jensen, USN
  Seaman 1st/c Gipe, USN
  Coxswain Franco, USN
ROYAL SAWBONES:
  Chief Pharmacist Mate Henningsen, USN
  Chief Commissary Steward Burkenbine, USN
ROYAL CORPSMEN:
  Baker 1st/c Beavers, USN
  PFC. Fulmer, USMC
ROYAL CHAPLAIN:
  Father Patrick, USN
ROYAL ALTAR BOYS AND CANDLE BEARERS:
  Steward Mate 1/c Scott, USN
CHAPLIN'S ASSISTANT:

Seaman 1/c Robinson, USN
ROYAL SCRIBES:
Radioman 1/c Richitelli, USN
Corporal Holman, USMC
ROYAL AIDES DE COURT:
Chief Boatswain Mate "Joe" Marcy, USN
Platoon Sgt. Miller, USMC

HIS MAJESTY'S ROYAL POLICE:
1st Sgt. Patterson, USMC and his force of 100 efficient and
highly trained United States Marine Corps
keepers of order.
Coxswain Lucas, USN and his force of fifty efficient and highly
trained United States Navy Custodians of
Order.

Of the over 1,000 members of the crew and passengers, less than 200 had been across the line before. Almost seventy-five percent of us were inexperienced seagoing novices.

My Individual Orders were:

Seaman Second Class Reding is hereby ordered to accompany Eggebrecht on all rounds dressed in a Red Sweater, Red Socks, Levi's rolled to the knees, Battle Helmet, one low slipper on the left foot and one field shoe on the right foot.

—By Order of His Royal Highness, King Rex.

How did they know? In March, when I went home on a three-day leave that they granted me after my appendicitis operation, I brought back aboard ship my red high school block sweater, a pair of red socks and my old Levi's jeans. When I went on liberty, I planned to take them ashore, change into them and—for a few hours—be a civilian high school student again. I had put them in my locker and never did get a chance to wear them. There certainly weren't any secrets aboard our ship.

Following King Rex's orders—in the tropical heat—I put on my wool high school sweater; red socks and faded blue Levi's jeans. It was great; I was the only civilian aboard the *Fergus*. But that didn't last long.

After going through the line leading up to the Tribunal that would deal with the sins of my past and future—known and projected—I was sternly informed that I was out of uniform and was ordered to discard such a bold costume that I had the effrontery to wear on a ship of the United States Navy. I was then to undergo the sacrifices necessary to make candidates worthy of entering the majestic world of the Golden Dragon, which was so wisely ruled by the benevolent King Rex.

Following orders, I went to my quarters, removed my outer civilian garments and returned to the fantail portion of the ship.

On the fantail, we were lined up and began the cleansing process. Ahead of us were the Royal Barbers who sheared all longhaired candidates to make them worthy to be received by His Majesty. The officers, and chief petty officers were excluded from this portion of the ceremony. Ah, the perks of rank.

We were then herded along in single-file lines toward large canvas chutes lying on the deck on the port and starboard sides of the ship. For the past two days, the Shellbacks—our masters—with the help of the chief commissary steward, had been accumulating soft mushy garbage like mashed potatoes, peas and scrambled eggs from the mess hall. In the tropics, the odor from this soft garbage quickly became ripe. On the morning of the ceremony, the strong-smelling gooey concoction was poured into the canvas chutes.

As Pollywogs, we were required to go into and through this smelly, mushy mess. Single-file, one at a time, in three-second intervals, we began to crawl on our hands and knees through the chute. Once inside the chute—to help speed us along—the Shellbacks began whacking the chute with pieces of medium-size manila hemp rope as paddles. It was a memorable, messy journey.

Upon emerging from the other end of the chute, we were greeted by the Royal Sanitation Crew with stinging seawater sprayed from one of the fire hoses. In the tropical heat, the seawater was a cooling, refreshing cleanser.

After being sheared and cleansed, the next stop on our journey to become Shellbacks was to the Royal Sawbones for our physical examination and medication.

Tables were set up near the forward and aft holds. I was at the aft hold. When it was my turn—with the aid of the Sawbones's Assistants— I was hoisted up on the table. The Assistants handled us like they were tossing cargo onto a loading platform.

My individual orders for the day.

Initiations of "Polly Wogs," May 1945. Clockwise from top left: King Neptune, Royal Baby, Royal Receiving Line, Royal Court.

Lying on the table, each Pollywog received a superficial external examination by the Sawbones's Assistants. Upon completion of the examination, the Sawbones—with the authority bestowed upon him—decreed that our present and future diseases required further cleansing.

As we lay on the table, we were ordered to consume a small potion of the "Royal Cleansing, Flushing and Healing Tonic," affectionately referred to as "Dragon's Breath."

Later we learned that ingredients for the concoction had been an aromatic mixture of horseradish, a touch of ground-up glue (for body), salt, cayenne pepper, Louisiana Pepper sauce, cloves, garlic, mustard, a touch of benzene, tunic pepper and Worcestershire sauce.

After having been sheared, cleansed, examined, and medicated we were considered worthy for presentation to the Royal Court. As we moved

Initiations of "Polly Wogs," May 1945. Clockwise from top left: Being presented to Royal Court, Emerging from garbage chute, Royal barber, Royal sawbones.

down the receiving line, we were presented to the Royal Baby. In the presence of the Royal Baby, we were required to bow, make "goo-goo" baby talk and kiss the top of his bristling GI-haircut head.

Next was the treat of all treats. We were presented to W.F. McGinnis, the Royal Princess. He was the saltiest-looking sailor aboard ship. Among the crew, McGinnis had a reputation of being the toughest, hardest-drinking, "fightingest" sailor on the ship. His face was a roadmap of years at sea and liberties in some of the roughest seaports in the world.

In the presence of such a noble person, we followed the protocol of graciously bowing and kissing the back of the Princess' hand. With a straight face, we had to—in detail—describe the beauty of the Princess' delicate features to the World of King Rex and the entire Universe. If any one of us smiled or laughed, Royal Guards would have us do ten push-ups.

At the conclusion of the ceremony, we were humbly presented to the Royal Mandarin. His Highness made the final decision as to whether we were worthy of entering his Kingdom of Neptune and to be forever-after known as Shellbacks, or if we were to be thrown into the ocean to be eaten by the sharks.

The Ruler was a kindly person. He benevolently bestowed upon us the honor and privilege of being proud members of His Hallowed Aquatic Kingdom. We were thereafter officially known as "Shellbacks." When the war was over, I understand that the Navy stopped the custom of having Pollywogs go through King Neptune's Court.

ENIWETOK, MARSHALL ISLANDS TO SAIPAN, MARIANA ISLANDS

A few days later we arrived at Eniwetok Atoll in the Marshall Islands. We were anchored in the lagoon off of Parry Island for two days before departing for Saipan in the Mariana Islands.

Leaving Eniwetok, we were in a convoy with the USS *Thomas A. Jefferson*, (APA 30), and the *USS Barnwell* (APA 132). Our escorts were the destroyer *USS Robinson* (DD 562) and the destroyer escort USS *Levy* (DE 162).

After we were underway and in our convoy formation, the captain made the announcement that our troops were replacement cadre for units engaged a battle for an island just south of the main Japanese islands of Kyushu and Honshu. The name of that island was Okinawa. Immediately following the announcement, the troops broke out their equipment and started to clean their rifles and sharpen their knives and bayonets.

I went topside and stood on the deck overlooking the fantail. A Marine Corporal in his early twenties walked up next to me. He had been in the Marine Corps for three years and had participated in the battles for Guadalcanal and Tarawa. Sitting below us was a squad of seventeen to twenty-year-old Marines intently sharpening their knives and cleaning their weapons.

Standing next to me, the corporal looked down at the young Marines. In a low voice, he said, "I hope that they never have to receive the 'Oh Shit Order.'" I looked at him and asked, "What do you mean? I've never heard of that one."

He looked grimly toward me and replied, "It means 'Fix Bayonets.'"

Looking into his eyes, I could visualize that the crude expression meant that your position was about to be over-run. The Marine's bayonet and knife would be his last-resort weapons for survival in hand-to-hand combat.

When we arrived at Saipan, the senior commanding officer was Admiral William H. Halsey, Commanding Officer of the Third Fleet. His flagship was the USS *Missouri* (BB 63). At Saipan, while we were taking on supplies, we were rammed by one of our own supply ships, LCT 982. A good-size hole was punctured into the hull of our ship.

At this time the battle for Okinawa could have gone either way. We were carrying troops that were urgently needed to reinforce our thinning forces on the island. The USS *Hocking* (APA 121) pulled up near us. Our marine passengers (17 officers and 688 enlisted men) were transferred to the *Hocking*. Then the *Hocking* immediately set sail on the relatively short but dangerous journey from Saipan to Okinawa.

BRINGING WOUNDED BACK TO THE STATES

After unloading our cargo and doing temporary repairs to our damaged hull, we sailed to Guam in the Mariana Islands. Vice Admiral C. A. Lockwood, on the USS *Holland* (AS 3) was the senior officer in command. Admiral Lockwood was the legendary COMSUBPAC, Commander of the Submarine Forces for the Pacific Fleet. His brilliant leadership helped our submarine forces sweep enemy shipping from the seas in the Central and Western Pacific Ocean.

We completed the repairs to our ship at Apra Harbor in Guam. We then received orders to transport casualties from the local naval hospital and other military personnel to the naval base at Pearl Harbor, Hawaii.

We left Apra Harbor with 456 passengers; 154 of them were casualties. Among the other passengers were ten officers and seventy-nine enlisted men being assigned to the Naval Combat Demolition School in the Hawaiian Islands. Graduates of the school became members of the UDT (Underwater Demolition Team), which later evolved into what is today known as the Navy Seals.

At Pearl Harbor, Admiral C. W. Nimitz was the senior officer in command. Docking near the submarine base, we disembarked the more serious casualties in need of immediate, additional medical treatment and the Navy personnel being transferred to the Naval Combat Demolition School. The less severely wounded remained aboard our ship.

After our passengers were unloaded and while we were replenishing our supplies, we began receiving 479 additional passengers for transportation to the States. Three of those passengers were prisoners (two marine privates and one sailor) that were being transferred to a naval prison. That same afternoon, we were underway. Once we had cleared the entrance channel to Pearl Harbor, the captain announced that our destination was San Francisco.

THE GOLDEN GATE

The shipping channel to San Francisco Bay was protected from enemy submarines and warships by a net made of steel cables. The barrier was placed seaward of the Golden Gate Bridge. Every evening at dusk it would be drawn across the channel. At dawn, small tender-boats would open the nets so that vessels could go into and out of the bay.

I can vividly remember June 24, 1945. We had arrived off the coast of California a few hours earlier, but had to "lay to" until after dawn. As soon as the nets were opened, we began our approach to the entrance to the San Francisco Bay. The sight of the Golden Gate Bridge silhouetted by the morning sun was spectacular.

As we slowly proceeded forward, a pilot—in his small, bobbing pilot boat—came out of the entrance of the Golden Gate and pulled up alongside us.

Pilots were licensed ship captains. They were specialists in local conditions regarding the tides, currents, navigational conditions and water hazards of their seaport. Most of the major harbors and seaports throughout the world had local pilots who boarded inbound or outbound ships to safely guide them into and out of the harbor.

We lowered a rope "Jacob's ladder" over the side. Timing the surge of the ocean with the movements of the two vessels, the pilot—with the agility of a circus acrobat—grasped the rungs of the swaying rope ladder and climbed up the ladder and over the rail. Safely aboard, he immediately went to the bridge, reported to the captain, and then, with the captain's permission, assumed command of the helm of the *Fergus*. Even though the pilot had command of the helm, the captain was still fully responsible for the ship. From the bridge, the pilot issued the orders, which would steer us through the passageway, under the Golden Gate Bridge and safety into San Francisco Bay. Our arrival was subdued and ghostlike.

Once we were inside the bay, two powerful stubby-shaped tugboats met us. With gentle nudges from their thick rope protected bows, we were moved to a dock at the Fort Mason Army Base. As we were being positioned alongside our berthing area, we saw some civilians and military personnel standing on the pier waving to us.

Then we heard the welcoming sounds of the Army Band playing songs like "Sentimental Journey" and "It's Been a Long, Long Time." The words and melodies of those two popular songs were a reflective yearning of what it would be like if the war was over and we could go home.

Even though we were in San Francisco Bay, we were still edgy and cautious. It was difficult to accept that we had actually returned from the war zone and could begin to relax. Being back in the "States" was great, but we still had a job to do.

After our lines were secured, we began disembarking the 143 casualties we were carrying (46 Navy, 33 Marine and 64 Army). Then the 302 other passengers went ashore. Watching the wounded being carried on stretchers or being helped off our ship was a somber, touching experience.

Some of our soldier, sailor and marine medical passengers were what the medics referred to as "walking wounded." They were suffering from what was called battle fatigue, or shell-shock. During the long journey across the Pacific, the battle-fatigue passengers would stand in the chow lines and move around the ship with blank stares on their faces. They performed the basic daily functions like the other passengers, but you could see that their minds were somewhere else. At a distance, they seemed normal. Even though they moved a little slower than most of the crew and other passengers, you would think that there was nothing wrong with them. But—as you got closer—you would see that the pupils of their eyes seemed to be larger, almost like they were dilated. One look and you knew that these passengers were different.

I wondered if those men were able to mentally and emotionally be healed from their hidden wounds so that they could return to the world of reality. For most of the physically and mentally wounded, the war was over. They would be going home. For us, it was back to sea.

SAN FRANCISCO TO SEATTLE

We were scheduled to do a quick turn-around and leave the next day.

No one received liberty. After disembarking our passengers we worked through most of the night replenishing our supplies and ammunition.

I went ashore and called my parents. It was nice talking to them. They were surprised that we were in San Francisco and were disappointed that they would not be able to see me. When I called my girlfriend, no one answered the telephone. I really wanted to see her, but since that was not possible, just to hear the sound of her voice would have been wonderful.

Early the next morning, June 25, 1945, we were underway to Seattle. The waters between San Francisco and Seattle were one of the roughest stretches that I had seen.

It was hard to believe, I was still only seventeen-years-old and had been in the Navy for over ten months. Almost seven of those months had been at sea aboard the *Fergus*. In April we took troops to the war zone, and now we were going back out there.

In Seattle, we docked along the waterfront and proceeded to take aboard 611 soldiers from the Army Base at Ft. Lewis, Washington. Again, we were in port just long enough to top-off our fuel and supplies, load our passengers and get underway. Our destination would be Okinawa.

The second night after we left Seattle, we lost a member of our crew. He was from the engine gang. Apparently he had received a "Dear John" letter from his wife. A Dear John was the name given to rejection letters that some fellows received from their wives or girlfriends. These unwelcome letters followed a basic format of how the women thought the men were wonderful, but they had gotten tired of waiting for them and had found someone else.

The Dear John received by the sailor on our ship was too much for him. The second night after we left Seattle heading west, he went topside. Someone saw him walk toward the fantail. In the darkness of the night, he disappeared. About the same time, we had another man who was so scared because we were going back to the war zone that he could not function. He was transferred off at the next port and sent to the hospital as a psychiatric case. They were casualties of the war.

CHAPTER VI

SUNDAY, AUGUST 12, 1945

OKINAWA
MY EIGHTEENTH BIRTHDAY

My eighteenth birthday was three days before the end of the war. A week after the war was declared to be over, censorship and diary restrictions were relaxed. I then started to write down where we were and began trying to piece together where we had been. Due to the International Dateline, the 11th of August in the USA was the 12th of August at Okinawa.

We had an air raid during the middle of the movie. My General Quarters station was as a telephone talker in a 20-mm ammunition-handling room in the aft portion of the superstructure.

If a shell or an airplane hit us in our area of the ship, the ammunition-handling room—with us in it—could go up like a giant bomb. In combat, being locked in an ammo-handling room was spooky.

As the talker, I was in communications with the CIC (Combat Information Center) and I could hear what was going on topside. They reported that a Kamikaze (Japanese suicide aircraft) or some type of explosive devise like a torpedo had hit the Battleship USS Pennsylvania (BB 38) in the fantail causing damage to the ship.

Also, Kamikazes sank a tanker and hit another APA (a troop ship like ours). They also said that the planes that attacked the Pennsylvania and the APA flew low right over us as they were looking for targets. We were lucky.

During our daily battle station practice drills, we would hear a calm voice on the ships public address system say, "General Quarters. General

Quarters. Man your battle stations," followed by the clanging of the ship's alarm. Under combat conditions—depending upon the time, place and conditions—the sound of the voice would have a more urgent, and sometimes even a frantic tone to it. Frequently the words "Man your battle stations" would be repeatedly followed by "This is no drill."

When we were in a combat zone, our minds and reflexes sharpened to a fine edge. Regardless of time of the day, when you heard the click of the button that activated the ship's PA system, you listened intensely for the orders that followed. If it was General Quarters, you would automatically start moving toward your battle station before the final syllables of "Quarters" was said. As soon as the general alarm sounded, the passengers were instructed to freeze in place and stand aside to make room for the crew to use the ladders and passageways. Under the intensely crowded conditions of having almost 700 passengers aboard ship, this reactive movement enabled our crew of almost 300 men to quickly move to our battle stations.

Before leaving Pearl Harbor, I wrote a letter to my mother, father, brother and sister. The letter was to be mailed to them in case we were hit and I was killed. I gave the letter to a shipmate, Melvin D. Norman from Payette, Idaho, whose battle station was up forward in the area of the bow. My combat station was aft near the stern. He gave me a letter addressed to his parents in case he was killed. Fortunately, neither one of the letters had to be mailed.

The first time we went to GQ and had Kamikazes flying over us, I was one scared seventeen-year-old sailor. I mean really scared. After a few air raids, I was a combination of being scared and angry. Some of my shipmates, who had been through combat before, said I was not alone. I should put it behind me, concentrate on doing my job and quit thinking too much.

The worst part was the waiting, the calm while you were in the eye of a storm with chaos swirling all around you. It was important to keep your mind focused. That was when the endless hours of drills became meaningful. We were so well trained that we reacted automatically.

When we were in a port at anchor in a harbor, we usually had three or four of our LCVP boats in the water tied to a boom that protruded from the side of ship near the forward hatch. In a combat area, these boats were equipped to make smoke with vaporized diesel fuel from smudge pots, similar to the type of smudge pots the farmers back home used to protect their fruit trees on frosty or freezing days.

When we were under attack by enemy aircraft, our boats would circle the ship, trying to create a large screen of smoke around us. Two of our boats would be used to produce the cloud, and a third boat would be used as standby, backup.

We were under orders not to fire at any enemy in the area unless they directly attacked us. The dark shrouds, which our smoke-boats created, were to hide us from the Japanese Kamikaze planes, submarines, and their small, agile suicide boats.

One of the reasons we were ordered not to fire at any enemy in the area was that our ammunition belts had "tracers" spaced in them. When rounds were fired at targets, the tracers in the ammo belts allowed the gunners to see the paths of the shells they were firing. If our gunners could see the path of the shells going toward the target, then the target could see where the shells came from.

When you are attacked your instincts are to retaliate to defend yourself. I just wished that we would have been allowed to strike back. But, we were troop transports, not warships. We didn't have the firepower to be gunfighters. We were instructed to use our guns only if the enemy was coming directly at us.

Aircraft carriers, large warships and transports with troops aboard were the Kamikazes' primary targets. After we unloaded our troops and cargo, we rode higher in the water. Theoretically, in daylight, our higher water line put us into a secondary target category. Theories are great as long as you are not part of the test.

The larger vessels like carriers and battleships, because of their size, were easier for those determined young Japanese pilots to see as they sought their final "targets of opportunity." In a life or death shoot- out, even though they were bristling with weapons which were capable of devastating firepower, our floating fortresses were still vulnerable.

Several anti-aircraft-guns were placed on our ship around the superstructure of the bridge where the captain and some of his key officers were located. The ammunition storage and handling rooms were usually positioned near the gun mounts. For attacking suicide pilots in their death dives, tracers that were being fired at them formed an ideal guide path to one of the more sensitive area of our ship.

Daily, we just sat there at anchor, trying to hide in the protective cloud covering created by our smoke-boats, and hoping that the Japanese pilots didn't decide to dive into our cloud. We did our job of bringing troops and supplies to Okinawa. Now we remained in the harbor at anchor, like target ducks in a shooting gallery. I wondered why.

THE FLEET THAT CAME TO STAY

Some of the old timers told us that in August 1942, the United States Marines invaded the Japanese held island of Guadalcanal. This was our first major offensive land action of the war. After the troops were ashore, due to heavy enemy naval opposition, our supply ships and support vessels withdrew from the area.

For several months, those tenacious Leathernecks were left in hostile territory with only our cargo carrying aircraft to provide them with the logistical supplies that were critically needed for a successful invasion campaign. In spite of the obstacles that were thrown at them, the Marines courageously prevailed and were successful in their conquest of the island.

Never again, in every operation after Guadalcanal, when our troops were landed on enemy shores, the fleet remained to support them. Remembering Guadalcanal, we were the fleet that came to stay.

I guess that's why we were held there. The Japanese pilots were not going to "banzai" our naval forces away from the island with their desperate Kamikaze—or any other—tactics. Reluctantly, it made sense.

USS *INDIANAPOLIS* (CA 35)

When we left the staging area at Ulithi Atoll in the Caroline Islands to go to Okinawa, we formed a convoy that was designated as UOK 45. Its commander was Commodore J.R. Palmer. He was aboard the USS *Riverside* (APA 102). The *Fergus* was the third ship in the second column, distance 700 yards, interval 1,000 yards.

The convoy consisted of thirty-seven ships (seventeen APAs, six AKAs and fourteen escort ships). The AKAs and APAs were carrying approximately 13,000 combat troops and their equipment.

I went up to the signal bridge to look around. In almost every direction from horizon to horizon, all I could see were ships. It was a powerful sight.

After we moved into our assigned convoy formation position, all personnel were cautioned that Japanese submarines were in the area and could be stalking us. Also, we were notified to be on the lookout for survivors or any signs of debris from a ship that was overdue and missing.

Months after the war was over, we learned that the missing ship was the cruiser USS *Indianapolis* (CA 35), more commonly known throughout the fleet as the "Indy." She had just completed a Top Secret high-speed cargo run from San Francisco, California to Tinian in the Mariana Islands. The cargo they delivered was the Atomic Bomb that was dropped on Hiroshima.

From the Marianas Sea Frontier, the cruiser was re-assigned to the Philippine Sea Frontier. In the early morning hours of July 30th, 1945, in the waters between Guam and the Philippines Islands, a torpedo that was fired from the Japanese submarine I-58 hit the USS *Indianapolis*. The warship reportedly sank in less than fifteen minutes.

According to the survivors, an estimated 300 to 400 of the crew went down with the ship. Approximately 800 men were supposed to have initially survived the sinking. As they floated in the warm tropical waters in life jackets and makeshift rafts, nearly 500 of them either drowned or were eaten by sharks. Only 316 members out of a ship's company of over 1,000 men were picked up alive.

We also heard that the destroyer escort USS *Underhill* (DE 682) had been sunk in the same area just a few days before the Indianapolis. The Underhill lost 119 men. At sea, you never knew what was going to happen. This was one of the reasons that most of us wore a sharpened, sheathed hunting knife. I didn't know how much protection a knife would be against a shark attack, but it might help.

MONDAY, AUGUST 13, 1945. OKINAWA

We expected to get it that night. The movie for the evening was "The Horn Blows at Midnight" with Jack Benny and Alexis Smith. Right after the movie started, General Quarters was sounded. The ships in Buckner Bay again seemed to be the primary targets.

The "scuttle butt" was that two APAs were hit. One sank when her boilers blew up. Even though the war was supposed to be almost over, Japanese aircraft were attacking us every evening.

They said that the battleship *Pennsylvania* (BB 38), nicknamed the

Pennsy, was not hit by a Kamikaze, but rather by a torpedo from a single Japanese plane (the one that flew right over us). The Pennsy reportedly received severe damage to the fantail portion of the ship and had up to twenty dead, and over ten wounded.

With the possibility of the Japanese surrendering within a matter of hours, if not days, plans were being put into action for the occupation of Japan. On the morning of August 12, 1945, Vice (three stars) Admiral Jesse B. Oldendorf transferred his flag from the battleship USS *Tennessee* (BB 43) to the *Pennsylvania*. Reportedly his staff and some VIP's accompanied the admiral when he relocated his command.

During the war in the Pacific, the *Pennsylvania* had participated in almost every major campaign from Pearl Harbor on December 7, 1941 to Okinawa. With such an outstanding combat record, it was scheduled to be one of the leading warships to sail into Tokyo Bay. They said that was the reason why the admiral transferred his flag to the Pennsy.

Also aboard the battleship on that fateful day was a young ensign named Johnny Carson from Norfolk, Nebraska. After the war was over he returned to college, went into show business and became a prominent the television talk show host.

Just prior to the 2045 (8:45 p.m.) deadly explosion, we heard that the Officers Of The Deck on the Pennsylvania were informed by their radarmen that an unidentified airplane was flying towards them.

With only one possible enemy aircraft in the area, the officers on duty reportedly didn't want to disturb the admiral and the VIPs. Therefore the general alarm wasn't sounded and the ship was not "buttoned up" for combat when that enemy plane made its deadly attack. If this was true, then those officers committed a serious breach of command responsibility.

The torpedo exploded into the fantail section of the ship, where most of the dead and wounded were in their living quarters preparing for bed, reading, writing letters or just lying around on their bunks.

Fortunately, the officers on our ship exercised due diligence. With the war supposedly almost over, someone had to be the "last one killed" in the conflict. We certainly didn't want it to be anyone on our ship.

We were able to hide the *Fergus* in the clouds created by our smoke boats. Battleships and carriers, with the height and the massiveness of their superstructures, were almost impossible to be hidden by a cloud of smoke.

With their awesome firepower, the best defense for battleships and carriers was suppose to be in open waters. There they could do their high-speed zigzag turns, and they had the weapons to shoot down attacking aircraft.

The enemy aimed another weapon at us. It was a radio broadcast from a woman who spoke perfect English. We called her Tokyo Rose. In a sensuous voice, from somewhere in Japan, she would broadcast American Big Band music interspersed with propaganda commentaries. It was nice to hear a female speaking English. We listened to the great music, and tried not to pay any attention to what she was talking about. At times her words would even bring smiles or chuckles from the crews.

PICKET SHIPS

During the final months of the war, as we moved closer to their homeland, the Japanese accelerated their efforts to destroy our fleet. Almost daily young Kamikaze suicide pilots took off from the southern-most islands of Japan to attack our ships that were in the waters off of Okinawa. It was almost impossible to defend a naval vessel against deter-mined aviators who were willing to crash their aircrafts into their targets. The only real defense was to shoot them down.

To protect our fleet, our Navy established a line of heavily armed anti-aircraft gun ships, known as "picket ships." With their firepower they formed an early warning perimeter line of defense as protection from the attacking aircraft. Most of these picket ships were destroyers, destroyer escorts and modified large landing craft such as LCIs (Landing Craft Infantry) and LSTs (Landing Craft Tanks). They were the ones that caught the initial lethal impact of the incoming waves of young suicide pilots.

In the midst of the carnage of battle a strange sense of humor emerged. In their weariness from fending off the banzai thrusts of the Kamikazes, some of the sailors on the smaller ships printed large multi-colored signs. These were drawn on sheets of cardboard or plywood. They had large cartoon sketches of battleships and aircraft carriers above direc-tional arrows. Printed below the arrows were phrases like, "Many big ships over there," or "That way for the highway to heaven." Thanks to the skill, courage and sacrifices of our picket ships sailors, many of us on ships in the waters around Okinawa survived the war.

TUESDAY, AUGUST 14, 1945. OKINAWA

Reports were to expect a heavy enemy attack any time that day. They said that a few days before, we dropped a second atomic bomb on Japan. In retaliation, the Japanese threatened to destroy the American forces on and around Okinawa. With the daily air attacks, we felt like stationary targets at a carnival shooting gallery.

That morning, when I was on the fantail, I counted over a hundred B-25 "Billie Mitchell" bombers take off and head north toward Japan. With their escort planes, there must have been 150 plus aircraft in that flight. Some of our air strikes on Japan were reported to have had over 500 aircraft in their formations.

The B-25 bomber was the same type of plane that Col. Jimmy Doolittle flew off the deck of the Carrier Hornet in his historic 1942 air raid attack on Tokyo. I don't see how he could have gotten such a large airplane off the carrier's relatively small deck.

Our boat crews were a good source of information for what was going on in an area. Most of them were former farm boys and they loved to talk. They picked up quite a bit of news and gossip from other boat crews while they were waiting to be loaded or unloaded during their shuttle runs back and forth between the ship and the beach.

One of the fellows said that there was a movie star named Tyrone Powers flying Marine transport planes into Okinawa from Guam or Saipan in the Marianas Islands. Powers was said to be a lieutenant in the Marine Corps and the pilot of the aircraft.

It was nice to hear of a movie star actually being out there with the rest of us, rather than being a "candy store hero" in Hollywood shooting make-believe war films. You had to hand it to him.

Also, when we were at Ulithi Atoll in the Caroline Islands, we heard that Bing Crosby's brother Bob Crosby was there. They said that he was an officer in the Marine Corps and the bandleader for a group of Marine Corps musicians. They were traveling around the islands entertaining the troops.

That night all hell broke loose. The word was passed around that the war was over. Everyone cut loose firing their guns. The people topside said they had never seen so many flashes in the sky. It was a false report. Some of men on the ships in the area and on the island were injured from falling shrapnel. You never knew what was going to happen. It certainly wasn't boring.

WEDNESDAY, AUGUST 15, 1945. OKINAWA

The captain announced that President Harry S. Truman had said that the Japanese accepted our unconditional surrender demand and the war with Japan was over.

You sure wouldn't know it around Okinawa. The night before, during the "false armistice," we'd had two air raids. The first attack was around 1900 (7 p.m.). The second attack was about 2200 (10 p.m.). For each attack, we were at our battle stations for better than forty-five minutes.

When the first air attack occurred, we had two of our LCVP boats in the water circling our ship, making protective clouds of smoke. In the confusion of hearing and watching enemy aircraft being shot at by our warships and ground fire from the island, one of our boats became lost in the clouds of smoke.

Not having any points of reference, our coxswain in the lost boat ended up circling an adjacent ship. Consequently, that ship had three boats circling it, making a thick protective cloud. We only had one circling boat attempting to create enough smoke with its smudge pots to hide us. The gusting sea breezes further diluted our protective cloud. For a while we were really vulnerable to the attacking Japanese pilots.

In my mind, I can still hear the voice from the bull horn on our ship urgently repeating, "Smoke boat 82, make more smoke . . . Smoke boat 82, make more smoke!" Later I heard that it was the captain himself, who almost frantically kept calling, "Smoke boat 82, make more smoke!" on the bullhorn.

The captain was angry with the coxswain who got lost. I don't know why our officers didn't have the usual backup boat in the water that day. It was poor planning; someone fouled up on that one. We were lucky.

Even though the war was supposed to be over, we went to General Quarters at 1900 (7 p.m.), an enemy aircraft flew within a mile of us and as usual, we were ordered to hold our fire.

After we secured from our battle stations, I was confused, we did not know what was happening. The Japanese were supposed to have surrendered; yet their aircrafts were still attacking us. The older fellows on the ship reassured us that everything would be all right. They had confidence that the war was really over.

Later that evening the captain gave a short speech over the public address system. He told us what a good crew we were and in celebration of this historic event we could "lay down" to the scullery where all hands would be issued a ration of two cans of beer. I helped to hand out the beer. I had never seen so many smiling happy faces. Some of the senior petty officers that had been in the Navy since the beginning of the war went to their lockers and broke out bottles of whiskey they'd been saving for this special day. There were smiles, laughter and yelling all over the ship. It was like being in a dream world . . . the war was over, and we were still alive. I had never heard so many ship's horns and whistles or seen so many searchlights. There were not as many guns being fired as there had been during the false armistice. The celebration seemed to be more subdued. It was hard to believe that maybe we would be able to go home. We wondered what it was like back in the States.

Later we learned that on Wednesday, August 15, 1945 the Japanese people had heard their Emperor's voice for the first time when he announced on the radio that the people of Japan should "endure the unendurable, and suffer the unsufferable" by laying down their arms, since Japan had accepted the terms to ended the war.

We also heard later that, on that same day, a Japanese admiral on the island of Kyushu—in direct defiance of the Emperor—ordered a bomber with a volunteer crew readied for a final Kamikaze attack on the American fleet at Okinawa. Over the strong objections of his aids, the admiral himself decided to fly the aircraft on its final mission.

When he arrived at the airfield, an entire squadron of aircraft was lined up with engines running. Volunteer airmen were standing by their planes. The admiral said that he had requested only one bomber. The squadron commander responded that every aircraft in the squadron would fly with him.

With the admiral in the lead aircraft, all of the bombers took off. Some of the planes had engine trouble and were unable to continue to their targets. Reluctantly, they returned to the base. The other aircraft proceeded on their banzai mission toward the American fleet in the waters off the coast of Okinawa.

At 1900 (7 p.m.), our radar picked up "bogies"—enemy aircraft—approaching Okinawa from Japan. We went to our battle stations. The Kamikazes didn't have radar; we did. Also, we were shrouded in the—hopefully—protective cloud of smoke made by our smoke boats. The attacking enemy aircraft flew within a mile of us. Hiding in our cloud of smoke, we were ordered to hold our fire.

At 1924 (7:24 p.m.), the admiral and the other aircraft commanders reportedly transmitted over their radios that they were crashing their planes into targets. We had more than one aircraft on our radar for a while, and then they disappeared. We didn't hear of any ships being hit. They could have been shot down because there was a lot of gunfire aimed at them.

THURSDAY, AUGUST 16, 1945. OKINAWA

After the Emperor's announcement of the cessation of hostilities, we remained at Okinawa, awaiting orders. Today, we started receiving cholera, typhoid and other shots. We thought that we might be going to Tokyo. I was glad that we would be carrying occupation—rather than invasion—troops to Japan. All sorts of rumors were being circulated. I didn't think that the captain or anyone else knew where we were going, or what they were going to do with us. We just followed the old military routine of hurry up and wait.

They said the APA that had been hit at Okinawa on August 12 was the USS *Lagrange* (APA 124). One of the Japanese Kamikaze Betty Bombers that had flown right over us had crashed into the *Lagrange's* bridge, killing twenty-one and wounding eighty-nine of its crew. Thank goodness for the thick clouds of smoke that our boats had created to hide us from the attacking aircraft.

We were restricted from going ashore. They said it was too dangerous. Only the boat crews, work parties and some officers had the opportunity see what it was like on the beach. The captain with some of our officers toured the island. When Lt. R.F. Tipton, one of the officers, returned to the ship, he told us about the some of interesting things that he had seen.

He said that Okinawans had suffered quite a bit from the conflict. But, in spite of the obvious carnage and the pall of death from the battle, he felt a sense of resiliency among the people. It was an interesting island. We were disappointed that we were not allowed to go ashore.

That night we finally finished the Jack Benny and Alexis Smith movie, The Horn Blows at Midnight. For the past three nights the movie had been interrupted by air raid attacks.

HIROSHIMA AND NAGASAKI

While we were waiting to find out where they were going to send us next, some members of the boat crews told us what they had heard about of the two atomic bombs and the fateful days when those two devastating weapons were dropped on Japan.

Through the subsequent years, as a result of my four visits to Saipan, in addition to conversations with Army Air Corps and U.S. Naval personnel who were on Tinian in August of 1945, the following basic information was received from the boat crews, confirmed and expanded upon.

Before dawn on the morning of August 6, 1945, a B-29 bomber named Enola Gay, with Colonel Paul Tibbets as the aircraft commander, took off from Tinian in the Mariana Islands with a secret weapon. The weapon was an atomic bomb made from uranium. It was named "Little Boy." The pilot had three potential target cities.

Several other aircraft also involved in the mission took off from Tinian that morning. One plane had instruments aboard to measure the force and intensity of the explosion, and the other was a photographic aircraft whose job was to take pictures of the explosion and the resulting damage. The first ones to leave the runway were the advance scout weather planes. Their job was to report the weather and other conditions over the targets. They reported that Hiroshima, the primary target, had a light overcast that was acceptable weather for bombing. Therefore, Hiroshima went into the history books.

At 0815, the Enola Gay was over the target. The bombardier's aiming point when he dropped the bomb was a bridge in the center of the city. Upon detonation, the explosive force and resulting incinerating blast of heat from that single weapon resulted in the death of over 100,000 people. Also among the possible casualties were Allied prisoners of war that were being held captive at the Hiroshima Castle Prison.

The Japanese government was again asked to surrender. The response was a stepping up of the Kamikaze attacks on our ships around Okinawa. Therefore, on August 8, 1945, a B-29 named Bock's Car took off from Tinian, piloted by Major Charles Sweeney. The aircraft carried an atomic bomb called "Fat Man." This device was made from plutonium.

Major Sweeney also had primary, secondary and tertiary targets. The primary target was Kokura, on the island of Honshu. The weather planes

FLASH - WHITE HOUSE - JULY 6. ATOMIC BOMB STATEMENT.

THE PRESIDENT TODAY MADE THE FOLLOWING STATEMENT: "SIXTEEN HOURS AGO AN AMERICAN AIRPLANE DROPPED ONE BOMB ON HIROSHIMA, AN IMPORTANT JAPANESE ARMY BASE. THE BOMB HAD MORE POWER THAN 20,000 TONS OF TNT. IT HAD MORE THAN TWO THOUSAND TIMES THE BLAST POWER OF THE BRITISH "GRAND SLAM", WHICH IS THE LARGEST BOMB EVER YET USED IN THE HISTORY OF WARFARE

SINCE 1939 IT HAS BEEN A RACE BETWEEN GERMANY AND THE COMBINED EFFORTS OF GREAT BRITAIN AND UNITED STATES TO ADD ATOMIC ENERGY TO THE OTHER ENERGIES OF WARFARE. THE GERMANS FAILED. WE MAY THANK PROVIDENCE THAT THEY GOT THE V1'S AND V2'S LATE IN THE WAR AND IN LIMITED QUANTITIES, AND EVEN MORE THAT THEY DID NOT GET THE ATOMIC BOMB AT ALL.

THE UNITED STATES HAD AVAILABLE THE LARGEST NUMBER OF SCIENTISTS IN THE MANY NEEDED AREAS OF KNOWLEDGE; WE ALSO HAD THE TREMENDOUS INDUSTRIAL AND FINANCIAL RESOURCES NECESSARY FOR THE PROJECT. BRITAIN WAS EXPECTED TO COOPERATE, BUT AT THE TIME WAS STILL UNDER THE POSSIBILITY OF INVASION. FOR THESE REASONS CHURCHILL AND ROOSEVELT AGREED THAT THE PROJECT WOULD BE DEVELOPED IN THE UNITEDSTATES.

OVER 65,000 INDIVIDUALS ARE EVEN NOW ENGAGED IN OPERATING THE PLANTS, MANY HAVE WORKED THERE FOR TWO AND ONE HALF YEARS. FEW KNEW WHAT THEY WERE PRODUCING. THEY SAW TREMENDOUS AMOUNTS OF MATERIALS GOING IN, AND NOTHING COMING OUT OF THESE PLANTS, FOR THE PHYSICAL SIZE OF THE EXPLOSIVE CHARGE IS EXCEEDINGLY SMALL. WE HAVE SPENT TWO BILLION DOLLARS ON THE GREATEST SCIENTIFIC DISCOVERY IN HISTORY, AND WON.

THE SECRETARY OF WAR, WHO HAS KEPT IN TOUCH WITH ALL THE PHASES OF THE DEVELOPEMENT, WILL MAKE A STATEMENT GIVING FUTHER DETAILS. HIS STATEMENT WILL GIVE FACTS CONCERNING THE PLANTS AT OAK RIDGE, KNOXVILLE, TENNESSEE, RICHMOND, VIRGINIA AND AT PASCO, WASHINGTON; AND AN INSTALLATION NEAR SANTA FE NEW MIXICO.

ATOMIC ENERGY MAY IN THE FUTURE SUPPLY THE POWER THAT NOW COMES FROM COAL, OIL, AND FALLING WATER, NOT THAT IT CAN BE PRODUCED ON A BASIS TO COMPETE WITH THEM. BEFORE THAT COMES THERE MUST BE A PERIOD OF INTENSIVE RESEARCH.

Received aboard USS Fergus *at sea, off of Okinawa. An error in transcription was made: July should have been August.*

reported that the city of Kokura was covered with a heavy overcast, therefore, the secondary target, Nagasaki, received the second atomic bomb. Over 70,000 people in Nagasaki died. It is an ironic coincidence that the torpedoes that sank the American ships at Pearl Harbor on December 7, 1941, were made at the Mitsubishi plant in Nagasaki.

FRIDAY, AUGUST 24, 1945.
EN-ROUTE-OKINAWA TO MANILA

We got underway at 1502 (3:02 p.m.) in accordance with Commander Amphibious Pacific Secrete dispatch #220350 of August 1945. Our destination was Manila Harbor, Philippine Islands. Once clear of the anchorage area, we commenced a zigzagging formation in accordance with Plan #23, USF 10.B.

Thirty-five minutes later we ceased zigzagging and joined Convoy # OKI 106. We were the lead ship in column 1. The USS *Catron* (PA 71), a twin stacker like the *Fergus*, was traveling with us along with two destroyer escorts, the USS *Cronin* (DE 704) and the USS *Gilligan* (DE 508). They were there to protect us from possible air or submarine attacks.

We still operated under wartime conditions of nighttime darkened ship along with Dawn and Dusk Alerts. The bow watch was on a high state of alert because we were in dangerous waters. Even though the war was supposed to be over, we didn't know what the millions of Japanese forces scattered throughout the Pacific Islands and the continent of Asia were going to do.

Later in the afternoon, after we had settled into our convoy formation, the captain announced that censorship was being relaxed. We could write to our loved ones and tell them where we were. But we shouldn't be too specific. We should just let them know our general location and that we were all right.

It was nice to be back at sea and going somewhere. Our estimated day of arrival in Manila was Monday, August 27th. The rumor was that we would pick up troops and go to Tokyo.

SUNDAY, AUGUST 26, 1945. AT SEA

We were cautioned to be especially aware of the possible presence of *loose floating mines. The day before, the United States Merchant Ship SS Peter White* was sunk by a mine in the waters off of Leyte in the

Philippine Islands.

Whenever we were topside—regardless of our job—we would visually scan the ocean for anything unusual. Topside, the standard procedure was eyeballs out; in other words, keep your eyes alert for anything in the sky and on or underneath the surface of the water that could be a threat to the safety of our ship.

That morning we saw a four-engine aircraft slowly moving across the cloudless sky near the horizon. I went up to the signal bridge and asked one of the signalmen what type of plane it was. He looked at his aircraft-recognition book and pointed to a picture of a B-17, which was a four-engine bomber.

I looked at the plane through the binocular-type telescope mounted on the signal bridge. It was really big, almost as large as the B-29's that we saw taking off from Saipan and Tinian in the Mariana Islands as they were heading north to bomb Japan.

This B-17 was different from the image in the recognition book. Under the fuselage, in the area that would have been its bomb bay, was a bulging item that looked like a boat.

I asked the signalman what was attached to the bottom of the fuselage. He took another look through the binoculars and said he also thought it was a boat. The signal officer came up and said that it was one of our four-engine long-range bombers that had been converted to a search-and-rescue aircraft. Modified with attached rescue boats, they were assigned the job of flying long distance patrols. The officer said that the B 17's were used primarily by the United States Army's 8th Air Force in the European Theater of Operations bombing campaign against Nazi Germany.

CHAPTER VII

MANILA, THE PEARL
OF THE ORIENT

Manila Bay was really big, the largest I had seen. As we entered the bay we saw Corregidor and Bataan. Corregidor was a pretty good-size island. You could clearly see the pockmarks of shell hole scars from the fierceness of the Japanese attack when they seized the island in the spring of 1942, and the residue from the battle when our forces recaptured this strategic location.

On February 16, 1945, to the surprise of the entrenched Japanese defenders, paratroopers from the U.S. Army's 503rd infantry suddenly descended upon Corregidor. The resulting combat was ferocious. The estimated 5,000 Japanese soldiers that were entrenched in the caves refused to surrender. Very few of them survived the subsequent struggle for the island. During the brutal battle our troops from the 503rd reportedly suffered up to twenty-five per cent casualties.

Corregidor, with its tadpole shape, was the largest of a series of small islands that guarded the entrance to Manila Bay. The total land area of the island was indicated to be about three and a half square miles, with the highest point being 450 feet above sea level.

From what I could see, it reminded me of one of the Channel Islands off the coast of California. The navigation chart indicated the island was about twenty-six miles from the city of Manila, which is about the same distance from Manila as Catalina Island is from Long Beach.

The Bataan Peninsula was rugged looking. I didn't see any clearings or open areas, just trees and dense jungle.

Our anchorage in the harbor was so far out in the bay that we were beyond the sight range of the city of Manila. The Navy had and probably still has a pecking order as to where ships are anchored or berthed. Warships were the prima donnas of the fleet. They came first, and then troop transports and auxiliary vessels. At the bottom of the order were freighters.

The USS *Riggs* (APA 110) was berthed right next to us. It was supposed to have been hit at Okinawa, but it sure didn't look like it. There was a battleship anchored about a mile away from us. They said it was the USS *Missouri* (BB 63).

President Truman was from the state of Missouri, and the word was that he was going to have the Japanese sign the peace treaty in Tokyo Harbor on the USS *Missouri* It made sense. Why not? Also, word was that General Douglas MacArthur was in Manila waiting to go to Japan.

I had never seen such a concentration of warships. With so many of them in the harbor we thought we were going to be part of the convoy to Tokyo. That would have been great.

Later, we learned that the battleship we saw was the USS *New Jersey* (BB 62) with Admiral Raymond Spruance aboard as the Commander of the 5th Fleet. Admiral Spruance was the commander of the fleet that had won the turning-point victory at the Battle of Midway. I didn't see the Missouri.

In addition to the anchorage pecking order, another reason we were located so far from the city was because of the sunken ships in the harbor. There must have been over a 100 of them. After hearing so much about Manila I sure hoped that they would allow us to go ashore. They said it was a fascinating city that was commonly referred to as the "Pearl of the Orient."

A typhoon was reported to be heading towards us. The captain decided that the ship would be safer at sea. He immediately ordered the setting of the "special sea detail." We pulled up our anchor, secured the ship for heavy weather and got underway.

The rest of that day and through most of the night we rode out the forces of nature with its gale force winds, high seas and very heavy rain.

Fortunately, we were on the perimeter of the typhoon and did not receive its full impact.

The next afternoon, when we sailed back into Manila Bay, the skies were blue and the water was placid—almost like glass. What a difference a day made. They said that it was typhoon season in this part of the world. The old timers said that they could really get destructive.

The movie that night—again—was "Thoroughbreds, Under Western Skies" starring Tom Neal, Adele Mara and Roger Pryor. It was the fourth time we had seen that movie. I had never heard of any of the stars. Also shown with the movie were the Pathé News and the Army-Navy Screen Magazine. They were usually interesting. At least we were able to see what had happened a few months ago in the rest of the world.

WEDNESDAY, AUGUST 29, 1945. MANILA BAY. THE SUNKEN TREASURES OF MANILA BAY

Today, two of our hardhat (steel-helmeted) divers were temporarily detached from our ship to a salvage crew working on the sunken ships in the harbor. The divers were specially trained volunteers and received extra pay for this hazardous duty.

One story was that the Japanese had plundered the gold and silver from the Philippine treasury. This trove of treasure was loaded aboard their merchant ships for transportation to Japan. Our forces sank the ships before they could leave the harbor. The other story was that Philippine Government Officials put millions of dollars worth of bullion aboard freighters and scuttled the ships in the harbor in order to hide the treasure from the Japanese. Take your choice as to which one was true. Either way, we sent our divers over to help recover the "Sunken Treasures of Manila Bay."

One of our divers, Motor Machinist's Mate Bobby McCammack, said that his diving team had located and retrieved some silver from one of the hulks.

The salvage operation to clear the sunken ships from Manila Harbor would be a monumental task. The skeletal remains of merchant ships were scattered all over the area. It looked like it would take years to clear up this residue from the war.

The captain had his Jeep taken ashore in one of our LCVP boats, which could be used to carry and land small vehicles like a Jeep. On the way to his gig the captain asked Lieutenant Junior Grade J.W. Cummins to go ashore with him. Being a junior officer, he immediately responded, "Yes sir!"

The coxswain of the LCVP boat later told us that once ashore, he watched the captain and the Lieutenant walk over to the Jeep. The keys were in the ignition. Mr. Cummins started to climb into the passenger's side of the vehicle. The captain motioned him over to the driver's side and said, "You drive."

He sheepishly looked at the captain and said, "I don't know how to drive."

The captain looked at him and said in a loud voice, "You don't know how to do what?"

He responded, "Sir, I have never learned how to drive."

Captain Snyder, bellowed back at him, "You are a lieutenant in the United States Navy and you don't know how to drive an automobile?"

Softly he replied, "Yes, sir. I attended a small college and couldn't afford a car, so I walked, rode my bicycle, rode with someone else or took public transportation. After graduation, when I married, my wife drove the car for us. As a college professor we had housing on campus, and I never took the time—or saw any reason—to learn how to drive."

The captain shook his head and told him to sit on the passenger's side. The captain then walked around the Jeep, sat on the driver's seat and started the engine. Before driving off down the unpaved road, the captain, with a disgusted look on his face, glanced over to the Lieutenant. Thus was the beginning of an interesting day in Manila. We were glad we were not in that Jeep.

Over five decades later, when he was almost eighty years old, I spoke to Mr. Cummins on the telephone. I asked him if the Manila story was accurate. He said, yes, and he never did learn how to drive.

THURSDAY, AUGUST 30, 1945
ANCHORED IN MANILA BAY

Twenty-five of our senior petty officers left the *Fergus* today for transportation to the nearest port of entry in the continental United States for discharge from the Navy. Most of the departing petty officers were in their early to mid-twenties and had up to three years of wartime sea duty. Some of them had not been home since they had completed boot camp.

Prior to the general announcement regarding their departure we were briefed on the rules and regulations pertaining to our obligation to the Navy and the criteria for separation from the service. The senior petty officers had either fulfilled their Regular Navy enlistment requirements, or, if they were Reservist, they had accumulated a sufficient number of points to be eligible for discharge from active duty.

When the war was concluded in August 1945, the United States Armed Forces had over 12,000,000 military personnel on active-duty. The post-war planning contained a program to return a majority of us back to civilian status.

To achieve this personnel downsizing in an equitable manner, a point system was established. We were informed that we needed thirty points in order to fulfill our obligation and become eligible for separation from the service.

Reservists were awarded one point for each month of active duty time plus an additional half point for each month spent overseas or on sea duty. Additional points were granted for combat decorations, such as the Purple Heart or Bronze Star. A Reservist with two years of sea duty would have the same number of points as a person with three years of stateside duty.

After the briefing, we became point-counters by adding the number of months that we had been on active duty and how many of them were sea duty. I had been in the Navy for one year, which would give me twelve points plus I had almost nine months of sea duty that would give me another four-and-one-half-points for a total of sixteen-and-one-half points.

Most of my shipmates that were about my age projected that we would need another eight to ten months aboard ship in order to accumulate a sufficient number of points to become civilians again. In the mean time we had a job to do. The departure of the senior petty officers left numerous voids in key duty leadership positions. There were quite a few slots open for us younger sailors to fill. Now it was our turn to step forward and run the ship.

MONDAY, SEPTEMBER 3, 1945

Manila harbor was a mess. There were sunken ships all over the bay, especially close to the city. The water depth in that area must have been

Manila Harbor 1945. Sunken merchant ships.

fairly shallow because the superstructures of many of the vessels were sticking out of the water.

The ride from our ship to the city's fleet landing near the mouth of the Pasig River was long and choppy. Our LCVP boats could operate in three to four feet of water. Even with such a shallow draft, our boats had to weave their way precariously through the hulks of sunken ships as they made their way to and from the fleet landing.

Today one of our LCVP boats—with a returning liberty party of twenty aboard—ran into a submerged object tearing a gash in the bottom of the boat. The coxswain got too close to a hulk of one of the sunken ships in the harbor. Luckily we had other landing crafts in the area. As the damaged boat began to fill up with water, it became partially submerged and settled on top of a portion of the superstructure of the ship that it hit.

One of our other boats carefully moved alongside, picked up the embarrassed, wet crew and the liberty party. Some of the members of the liberty-party were in wobbly shape from too much of the beer and whiskey served in the bars of Manila. Fortunately no one was hurt. We sent over a salvage crew on one of our other LCVP's. They patched up the damaged craft and towed it back to our ship.

Old-time, regular Navy coxswains rarely if ever got into trouble with their boats. The coxswain of this LCVP boat was a reservist that had just recently been promoted. His inexperience was obvious. After a hearing was held, he was demoted and was back on the deck-force chipping paint.

After going through the stress and dangers of months of being together at sea under wartime conditions, our crew developed a special bond. We felt responsible for helping and taking care of each other.

BOOZE AND THE BEACH

For inexperienced teenage sailors, booze and the beach most of the times meant trouble and could even be a lethal combination. I had some problems when I went ashore at Ulithi Atoll in the Caroline Islands. We had a ship's softball game on Mog Mog, the fleet recreation island. On each base we put a case of beer. If you got onto first base, you could have a drink of beer, and so forth around the bases.

I was a pretty good baseball player. Getting a hit every time I batted resulted in frequent visits to the bases. In that tropical heat with a warm beer on each base, after a few innings most of us didn't know what type of game we were playing, nor did we care.

The fleet landing was located at one the temporary piers that jutted into the lagoon from Mog Mog's sandy shoreline. Liberty boats from the ships in the harbor pulled up to the fleet landing pier. With loose tether lines they tied up adjacent to each other.

An hour or so before our liberty was up we started moving towards fleet landing. I was with several of my shipmates as we staggered out onto the pier looking for one of our boats.

Our ship's designation and number were APA 82. The number and designation were painted in large letters on port and starboard sides of the bows of all of our boats along with each boat's individual number. We spotted PA 82 on one of the LCVP boats (PA is an abbreviation for APA) and headed towards it.

With its engine idling, our ride was moored outboard of a boat from another ship. Norbert D. Franxman from Covington, Kentucky was the coxswain.

As I wobbled across the gunwales of the LCVPs, swells created by the wakes of incoming and outgoing crafts caused the boats to move with the surges. I lost my balance and fell between two of them. The crews had fenders out to prevent the two vessels from bumping into each other, but a human head and body was larger than the fenders.

As I hit the water, Franxman instinctively threw our boat into reverse, backing it down. His quick reaction moved our vessel back far enough to provide sufficient space for the two boats to bump together without crushing my skull. Two of my shipmates reached over the side, grabbed hold and pulled me out of the water. If it had not been for Franxman's quick reflexes, my mother would have received that dreaded telegram saying that her seventeen-year-old son had been killed in the Western Pacific war zone.

TUESDAY, SEPTEMBER 4, 1945, AT ANCHOR IN MANILA HARBOR

Our ship's newspaper, the *Fergus*ette that was better known as the Snooze, tried to keep us up to date on what was happening in the world. But the news was almost always stale and filtered.

The only time I read the unfiltered story about what was going on at home and the rest of the world was when I heard from my mother. She was really great about writing. When we were underway, which we had been for most of the year, it usually took anywhere from a month to three months for our mail to catch up with us. It had been over a month since we had our last Mail Call. Hopefully, those elusive mail sacks were out there somewhere.

LIBERTY IN MANILA

Manila, the largest city in the Philippine Islands, was known throughout the world as the Pearl of the Orient. Its beautiful Walled City dated back to the sixteenth century when Spain controlled the archipelago. In February-March 1945, this historical heart of Manila was almost completely destroyed by the ferocity to recapture it from the occupying Japanese forces.

The battle resulted in intense shelling, bombing and street fighting. As a result, many of the beautiful buildings along the Pasig River and in the center of the town were heavily damaged or reduced to piles of rubble.

I made liberty every other day, which was more of a challenge than a pleasant experience. More than any other port that we visited, Manila was an adventure in survival. As we left the ship to go ashore, we showed our ID card and liberty pass. Then we were handed a pro-kit. The pro-kit contained a condom and a small tube of antibiotic cream to be used if the sailor should fall under the spell of the rapture of the Philippine females.

We were told that the water ashore was not drinkable so we were also allowed to carry drinking water in our personal canteens, which we wore on a web belt around our waist. Also, we were briefed that we should beware of counterfeit money. The Philippine peso, which had some minimal value, had the word VICTORY printed on the backside of the bills. The Japanese also had paper money that they had used during the period of occupation. That money also was in pesos, but it was now worthless.

The fleet landing was located near the mouth of the Pasig River where it flowed into Manila Bay. The stench of animal droppings, garbage, and just the foulness of the aftermath of war, permeated the air. The smell was so strong that it could be detected quite a distance out into the bay.

Adjacent to the fleet landing were hundreds of local people milling around their open-air flea market type of stands waiting for sailors to

come ashore.

The looks in the eyes of those brave Filipinos reflected the painful misery that they suffered during the years of the Japanese occupation, and the violence of the fighting to drive the enemy from their homeland. We heard that over 100,000 Filipino residents of Manila had been killed during the occupation and in the recent battle to recapture the city. They were so appreciative to see Americans.

In this atmosphere, the most popular items used for bartering were cigarettes, candy and clothing. The most sought-after was U.S. cigarettes. A carton of cigarettes, which cost us fifty cents at our ship's store, could buy almost anything in the city of Manila. Since they seemed to be in such a high demand for exchange, we tried to bring a carton or two with us when we went ashore in foreign ports.

One of the first things a sailor on liberty heard as he walked away from fleet landing was "Pomb Pomb Joe?" Young eight, nine, and ten year old Filipino boys would follow you around, asking "Pomb Pomb Joe? Take you home to my mother, my sisters, Pomb Pomb. All virgins, Joe. Just one carton of cigarettes." I had never seen such a heavily populated country with so many virgins. Welcome to shore leave in an exotic port.

After a few beers, four of us from our ship-for a carton of cigarettes each-finally said okay to a couple of young kids hustling the females in their families.

For two packages of cigarettes—costing ten cents—we climbed aboard a Philippine taxi, which was a small, covered, colorfully decorated, two-wheeled horse drawn cart. The youngsters climbed aboard with them. Off we went on a bumpy ride down a muddy, pothole-strewn road to their home.

The house was a one room wooden-framed structure that was constructed on stilts, which were four to five feet off the ground. The building was typical of the other residences in the area. It had pandanus mat walls and a palm-frond thatched roof. Small Chickens with colorful feathers ran all around the property and were perched on the steps that led from the muddy yard to the small porch in front of the woven pandanus mat doorway.

The windows—called eyebrows by Americans—were rectangular cutouts in the mat siding. Wooden sticks propped open the eyebrows. This allowed the trade winds to flow through the room and help give some relief from the oppressive heat and high humidity of the tropical Philippines.

In the house were the grandfather, grandmother, the mother, her two nineteen to twenty-year-old daughters, and several smaller children.

Hanging from the rafters, in a corner of the room, were several kaki-colored U.S. Army blankets. Behind the blankets was the privacy area of the house. There the girls, one at a time, would entertain their guests for a carton of cigarettes per customer. It was survival in the aftermath of the ravages of war.

MANILA, THE REAL WILD WEST

On one of my liberties in Manila, I was caught up in an incident, which really soured me on going ashore. Because of the danger, we were allowed liberty only during daylight hours.

Manila, 1945. The city in ruins, and refugees returning to the city.

U.S. Army soldiers were almost everywhere. Most of them were still wearing their combat gear and carrying weapons. We were told that the Army was conducting patrols up in the nearby mountains. Almost every day, the patrols would flush twenty to fifty Japanese soldiers out of the jungle.

The city was fairly safe during daylight hours if we stayed relatively close to the fleet landing. But nighttime was a different story. It was too dangerous. We had to be back aboard ship before sundown.

Near the fleet landing, some of my shipmates and I had been in an open-air tropical bar which had hand-operated ceiling fans. We were having some local beer, which we had been told was safe to drink. I think it was called San Miguel Beer.

Suddenly, three American soldiers with carbine rifles came into the bar and started yelling and firing shots into the ceiling. It was like something out of a Western movie, only these were soldiers not cowboys, and the bullets were real.

We dived under the table. The soldiers looked like they were drunk or high on something. It got spooky. People were yelling, screaming, and running around. As soon as we could, we got out of the area and headed back to the fleet landing.

That was the last time I went ashore in Manila. I didn't want to have gone through the war only to end up getting killed while drinking beer in a tropical saloon. I had never thought that I would ever give up a chance to make liberty, but the city had such strong, unpleasant odors, it was actually a pleasure to stay aboard ship. I was glad that I was a Sailor, not a Soldier, or a Marine. For the rest of the time that we were in Manila Harbor, I remained aboard the *Fergus* and caught up on my sleep.

TUESDAY, SEPTEMBER 4, 1945
MANILA HARBOR, CENSORSHIP IS REMOVED

Our ship's newspaper said that censorship regulations had been lifted for ships east of the International Dateline (180 degrees longitude). They said that any ship west of the dateline was still under censorship. We were several thousand miles west of the dateline.

When we were at Okinawa, a few days after the war was supposed to be over, the captain had said that we could write home and tell our families where we were. A few weeks later they said that censorship was still

Street scenes at Fleet landing, Manila 1945.

in effect. Typical military—they told us one thing, and then they told us just the opposite. I hoped my letters went through all right.

Censorship rules and regulations were emphasized from the moment we began our indoctrination as brand new recruits in boot camp. We were under specific restrictions as to what could and could not be disclosed. We were constantly being reminded and cautioned to be careful that even the slightest bit of information about our ship might be helpful to the enemy. Each page of our letters had to be signed with our full name, rank and duty division.

On the *Fergus*, every bit of correspondence was read before it left the ship. The censors were usually junior grade officers (ensigns or lieutenant jgs). If they thought that any word, phrase or mark were contrary to the basic censorship regulations, the violations were cut out with scissors. My mother received several of my letters with sentences and paragraphs removed.

We knew what was going on immediately around us. Even though we were in the war zone, we knew we were all right. For our families and loved ones back home, it was different.

Receiving letters from us that were weeks to months old with words or sentences blacked out or cut out, let the folks back home know that we were in harm's way, but they didn't know where.

The seldom-mentioned emotionally draining aspect of war was for our families to read newspaper reports of battles and hear about casualties without knowing where we were, or if we were all right. The not knowing for the prolonged periods of weeks to months between letters must have been difficult to handle.

SCUTTLEBUTT

Scuttlebutt (gossip, hearsay, and actual experience) is the information network among sailors on the ships of the fleet. It was amazing. Overall the news and information that traveled through the scuttlebutt pipeline was fairly accurate.

Whenever we pulled into port, we would put some of our LCVP boats into the water. They were used as our water taxi, cargo carriers or almost everything else that could be done on the water in a harbor. The boat crews were busy in the way they got around. They were like little bugs moving about a large pond. When they returned to our ship, one of the first things they wanted was a cup of joe and a bite to eat from the galley.

Ship's cooks were usually the first to talk to the returning boat crewmembers. I would ask them, "What's new?" That would be all they needed. The scuttlebutt that they picked up from the other ships would pour forth. Some of it was off-base, but most of the information was pretty accurate.

Between the scuttlebutt from the boat crews and the radio shack, usually the cooks in the galley knew what was going on before the captain and the officer of the deck.

There was a pecking order aboard ship. The boatswain's mates, gunners, quartermasters and signalmen thought they were the chosen few. In actuality, the cooks were at the top of the pecking order. Food was very important to sailors at sea. The cooks had the food.

When a non-classified message was received in the radio shack, the duty radioman would make an extra copy for the cooks. He would drop off our copy at the galley while he was delivering copies to the captain and the officer of the deck.

THE DEATH OF ERNIE PYLE

While we were anchored in Manila Harbor, Radioman First Class Louis E. Richitelli, from Connecticut, saw me reading Ernie Pyle's book *Here is Your War*. He told me that Pyle had been killed on a small island named Ie Shima, located near Okinawa. He wondered if I was interested in having a copy of a news report that he had in his files telling how, when and where the author had died. It was a shock to hear that Pyle was dead. After what he had been through, he seemed invincible.

I enjoyed reading his newspaper articles and his books. In fact, later when I enrolled in college, I became a journalism major with the hopes of becoming a correspondent like Ernie Pyle.

I said, "Definitely yes!" Then I asked Richitelli why the ship's newspaper had not reported this sooner. He said, "Ernie Pyle was killed last April, a few days before President Franklin Roosevelt died. Roosevelt's death and funeral so dominated the news, that the correspondent's death was overshadowed." With the passing of time and the magnitude of subsequent world events, Pyle became just a few newsworthy lines that were filed away in the history of the era.

The correspondent was noted for his style of graphically yet tastefully describing the everyday events of the war. Most reporters wrote about the major aspects of the conflict, or the high-profile officers and their feats. Pyle had the unique ability of relating the story of the ordinary enlisted man and the daily drudgery the "grunts" went through in the deadly process of fighting or helping to fight our country's battles.

He covered almost every major campaign in the European Theater of Operations. To the troops, Ernie was affectionately known as "the GI Journalist." When the European conflict was winding down, he came to the Pacific, where he was killed.

The report said that on April 17, 1945, the day after we invaded Ie Shima, an island near Okinawa, Ernie Pyle went ashore with some other correspondents. Ie Shima had three airstrips, which were needed as bases for our aircraft to help win the battle for Okinawa. Ernie was an infantryman's correspondent. As a battlefield veteran, he was well aware that even the smallest mistake could be fatal.

The account we read was that on the morning of April 18, Ernie and some of the other reporters were briefed on the status of the battle. Wanting to be closer to the action, he hopped a ride on a Jeep heading for the front. With him were two officers and a radioman with his field radio. The radio had a large antenna. Jeeps and trucks carrying radios with their long antennas usually indicated that a command officer was riding in the vehicle. That morning several Jeeps and trucks had safely moved along that road toward the front without any problems.

The Japanese had a tactic of moving snipers with rifles or automatic weapons behind our lines at night. These snipers would hide in caves, behind rocks or in bushes within gunshot range of roads or paths. They would patiently wait before firing what could be their final shots. Their primary targets were officers—the higher the rank, the better.

At a junction in the road, a sniper with an automatic weapon saw the Jeep with its long radio antenna and started firing. The driver slammed on the brakes. Pyle along with the other occupants of the vehicle hit the ground and dove into a drainage ditch along the side of the road. After that initial burst of gunfire, things were quiet.

As a combat veteran—lying in the shallow drainage ditch—he should have known better, but curiosity clouded his judgment. He raised his head to determine the status of the situation. The Japanese sniper fired again. A bullet struck Pyle in the head, instantly killing him.

He certainly had a gift for words, and an understanding of the hardships endured by the troops on the ground and the sailors of the fleet. He was originally buried in the temporary American military cemetery on Ie Shima. After the war was over, his body was relocated to the Punch Bowl National Military Cemetery near Honolulu on the island of Oahu.

CHAPTER VIII

TACLOBAN, LEYTE, PHILIPPINE ISLANDS

MONDAY, 10 SEPTEMBER 1945
AT SEA, EN-ROUTE TO TACLOBAN

We left Manila for the island of Leyte. No more darkened ship—we ran with our lights on and the hatches open. It was nice to get a better circulation of air into the ship. The tropical weather was hot and humid. The air below was stuffy.

I had been at sea for almost a year and it seemed strange to go topside at night and see lights on our ship and other ships in the area. We no longer had to grope around in the dark or rely just on the light from the moon. Moonlight had been a double-edged sword. It made it easier for us to see topside and it also made it easier for a submarine to see us. It looked like the war was really over. It was hard to believe. We still stood watches looking for mines and floating obstacles. The fighting might have been over, but the dangerous residue from the conflict was still out there.

The scuttlebutt around the ship was that when we were traveling from Okinawa to Manila, some of the officers had slept in for Dawn Alert. The captain was not happy about it. He confined the officers to their quarters.

After hearing the story, I was curious to find out the details behind the officers' decision to become temporary civilians. I asked one of their steward mates, Farragut A. Flippins, Steward's Mate Second Class, what had happened.

The steward mates were the waiters in the officers' wardroom. They would overhear conversations while serving the meals. They often knew as much, and sometimes more, about what was happening on the ship than the captain.

Flippins, as a fellow cook, relayed to me what he had heard regarding the incident. Since the war was suppose to be over, Dr. Cazan, Lieutenant N. H. McManus, Ensign R. D. Loutzenhiser, and Marine 2nd Lieutenant J. Kutzen, opened the portholes in their rooms for a better flow of fresh air. Since we were still under blackout conditions, they unscrewed the light bulbs in their quarters so that the lights would not accidentally be turned on during the night. No one woke them up at 0400 (4 a.m.) and they slept through the Dawn Alert.

The captain sternly reprimanded them and emphasized that officers were supposed to set an example for the rest of the crew. Their conduct was expected to be beyond reproach. As punishment, the four of them were relieved of their duties for five days and were restricted to the ship at the next port.

When we sailed from Manila, two members of our crew, Boatswain Caro and Coxswain Franxman, were not aboard ship. We wondered what had happened to them. We hoped they were all right.

I did not envy the captain. Trying to deal with his officers and crew would be like attempting to herd several hundred cats. Captain Snyder was an interesting person. We heard that he had graduated from the U.S. Naval Academy in the early 1920's. That was when the World War I fleet was being deactivated and downsized to a skeleton of its wartime force.

After graduation, they said there was an overabundance of junior grade officers in the Navy. He went into the reserve forces and returned to civilian life. As a civilian, he went to podiatry school where he received a doctorate degree.

He stayed in the reserves and through peacetime training attained the rank of commander. When the war started, he was called to active-duty. The *Fergus* was supposed to be his first command. As the captain of the *Fergus*, he had a new ship that was manned primarily by inexperienced personnel. He molded us to be highly competent crew. It was a good ship. We thought that we were the best in the Navy.

The captain was about five foot ten and had a thin Errol Flynn/Clark Gable-type mustache. He was a sharp-looking naval officer and wore the stripes of a full commander with dignity and a flair.

My shipmates seemed to either like him, or could not stand him.

Maybe that was the price of leadership. Being in command of a United States Naval vessel is reported to be one of the loneliest jobs in the world. As the captain he is fully responsible for the ship, the crew and its passengers. It takes a special type of person to be able to successfully handle life and death command decisions.

When we were at our special sea detail stations, I was the captain's runner. This meant that I stood by on the bridge to personally deliver messages for him or other officers on the bridge if the other types of shipboard communications broke down or were unavailable. To me, he was okay, but I tried to stay as far away from him as I could.

WEDNESDAY, SEPTEMBER 12, 1945. AT SEA EN ROUTE FROM MANILA, LUZON TO TACLOBAN, LEYTE

I had never seen such clear water. Everywhere you looked in this hot, humid climate, there were tropical islands covered with lush green foliage. This was a beautiful area of the world. They said that there were 7,083 islands in the Philippine Archipelago.

Thank goodness we ran with the hatches open for better air circulation. The tropics could really be a bear, especially at night when we ran under blackout conditions with the ship buttoned up. We had sixteen cooks sleeping in our compartment. For the sixteen of us, our total living area including bunks and lockers was ten feet by twenty feet.

After the war was over and conditions were more relaxed, I was able to sleep topside in the refreshing ocean breezes rather than in the hot stale air of my bunk in our crowded quarters.

I tied my hammock to the metal support legs underneath the aft starboard gun tub. At night, I would lie there and look up at the beautiful tropical moon in the clear starlit sky. The rolling motion of the ship would rock me to sleep. It was really great.

We all were wondering why we were going to Tacloban and where we were going afterwards. On the day the war was supposed to be over, we were at Okinawa near Japan. Since then, we had been gradually moving farther and farther away from the Japanese homeland. The military certainly had strange ways of moving us around like pawns on a chessboard.

THURSDAY, SEPTEMBER 13, 1945
SAN PEDRO BAY, TACLOBAN, LEYTE, PHILIPPINE ISLANDS

We arrived at Tacloban three days after we left Manila. The large busy port was located on the island of Leyte. The area was beautiful with its lush green foliage. All I could see beyond the shoreline beaches were dense jungle and mountains. The Army must have had a difficult time taking this island.

With all of the activity of the ships in the harbor and the quantity of supplies on the beach, Tacloban was definitely a staging area for the stepping-stone invasion path along our route to Japan.

Our mooring location was offshore from Red Beach. As soon as we dropped our anchor and even before we were secured from our Special Sea Detail, Filipino men, women and young boys in small hand-made outrigger canoes began paddling towards our ship. Although the war was supposed to be over, our daily routine was still based on wartime conditions. Our officers didn't like unfamiliar small boats, or anything else, moving within a comfortable defensive radius of our ship.

On deck, we had armed guards carrying rifles with live ammunition stationed at key positions around the perimeter of the ship. They were instructed to keep all unauthorized boats or boarding parties at a safe distance.

In spite of warnings, the Filipinos in their outriggers began slowly floating in closer to us. We motioned for them to keep their boats away from the ship, but not with the authority we would have used if we thought they were a threat. After what they had been through, the rules were relaxed.

When they had floated to within easy visual distance from our ship, the small boats turned into a floating flea market. They tried to sell us anything they had. The women held up trinkets and artifacts.

We were not allowed any contact with them. Therefore, we were unable to purchase any of their artifacts. But, we did toss coins or packages of cigarettes toward them. It was amazing to see the young Filipino boys instinctively move towards the projected landing spots. With the agility of experiences hunters, they would catch the objects in the air or dive into the water and retrieve them before they sank below the surface.

Jimmie Golden, Captains "Gig" and Philippine paddle canoes. Talloban, Leyte 1945.

They were survivors. After almost three years of being subjected to the harshness and brutality of the Japanese occupation forces, they could still smile and laugh. The Filipinos were very nice. They seemed to really like Americans.

The USS *Fillmore* (APA 83) was here. She was one ship behind us. There were a couple of fellows on the 83 that had been in boot camp with R. V. Little and myself. R. V. and I asked the officer of the deck if we could visit friends on the 83. The OD said okay, if we could find a ride. With all of the activity of our boats, we got one to drop us off at the 83 and later pick us up. We had a nice visit. It certainly was a small world.

GENERAL DOUGLAS MACARTHUR

Less than eleven months earlier, on October 20, 1944, a U.S. Naval amphibious task force landed General Douglas MacArthur and his troops on the beaches at Tacloban, Leyte. With showmanship and determination, the General fulfilled his promise to the people of the Philippine Islands that he would return. On that date, the deadly land campaign to drive the Japanese army from the Philippine Islands began.

Four days later, from October 24th to the 26th, 1944, a fierce naval battle was fought in Leyte Gulf for control of the Philippine Sea. The outcome of that action was a major factor in the success of the invasion landings on Leyte and the other islands in the archipelago.

The Filipinos thought highly of General MacArthur. That sentiment didn't necessarily prevail for the American soldiers who served under his command. Some of them called him "Dugout Doug" (dugout for the native hand-made canoes), which referred to his escape from the Japanese in 1942, when they seized the Philippines. Also, he was called "Duck Out Doug" because he left his troops and ducked out to Australia with his wife and his son.

Actually, according to what I heard and read, General MacArthur was ordered to leave the Philippines by President Roosevelt, our country's Commander-In-Chief. MacArthur's long and dangerous journey from the Philippines to Australia began in Manila Bay on the island fortress of Corregidor. In the early evening of March 11, 1942, the General and his party boarded Lieutenant John D. Bulkeley's PT 41. In a convoy with three other PT boats, they began the hazardous, elusive nighttime run through mine fields and Japanese blockades.

With Lieutenant Bulkeley's boat in the lead, the craft hid by day and traveled by night as they headed south toward the island of Mindanao in the southern Philippines. Upon reaching Mindanao, which was still controlled by our forces, the General and his party flew to Australia.

MacArthur was a remarkable and controversial leader. He had a flamboyant style with his distinctive cap and his corncob pipe. During the darkest hours of the war, the General's determined pronouncement of "I shall return" was broadcast over the Philippine Voice of Freedom Radio. His bold statement gave the Filipinos hope. They respected him and he didn't let them down.

Some of the fellows that had been at Tacloban since MacArthur's dramatic landing told us that the General's staff had planned a Grand Returning. They scheduled a media-covered event on a small, temporary pier that had been built at Red Beach. With hundreds of landing craft moving about the area unloading troops and supplies, his VIP boat—carrying the President of the Philippines and several generals—got caught up in the confusion of the heavy boat traffic.

A member of the General's staff radioed ashore to the beachmaster, a U.S. naval officer. The beachmaster was in charge of a designated area of the combat landing zone. He decided when and where troops and supplies were brought ashore on his beach. The General's staff member requested that all boats be cleared away from the temporary pier so that the General and his party could land there.

Whoever answered the request informed the General's staff member that Red Beach was in the middle of an invasion landing. They were trying to get troops and supplies to the combat commanders as quickly as possible. The pier was needed for critical items, which could not be unloaded on the sandy beach. "If the General and his guests want to come ashore," he said, "let them land in the surf and walk through the water like everyone else."

Therefore, the famous photographs of General Douglas MacArthur and his group of VIPs returning to the Philippines went into the history books showing them wading ashore through the surf instead of stepping off of a landing craft onto a temporary pier. Historic incidents have strange ways of occurring.

MacArthur was a controversial, inspirational leader who was at the right place at the right time.

SATURDAY, SEPTEMBER 15, 1945. RED BEACH TACLOBAN, LEYTE, PHILIPPINE ISLANDS

Since we had dropped anchor, the boat crews had been making runs back and forth to the beach, loading and unloading troops and their cargo. Most of the crews had been sleeping in their boats. Occasionally they would come aboard for chow. Some of them had not had six hours of sleep in over two days.

In order to give them a few hours of rest, sailors from the other divisions relieved the boat crews on a rotation basis. Last night, for a few hours, I was a motor-mac in charge of the engine. I didn't know what we would have done if something had actually happened to the motor. Also, I drove an LCVP boat for a while. It was fun being a coxswain. I was a teenager with a big toy boat.

We brought aboard more cargo than we could have ever imagined that she could carry. For over forty-eight hours, boats and outboard-type-motor-driven barges pulled along the port and starboard sides of the *Fergus* to unload their cargoes. A steady flow of K rations, beer, ammunition, gasoline, hospital supplies, trucks, jeeps, guns and troops were loaded aboard. We reached and exceeded our recommended maximum carrying capacity.

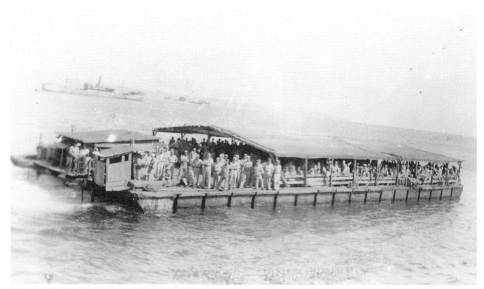

Troops being transported to our ship. Talloban, Leyte 1945.

The scuttlebutt was that we would soon be getting underway in a large convoy to go to some island in northern Japan.

Whenever we pulled into a forward area, the crew was usually restricted to the ship. The only ones allowed to go ashore were members of the boat crews and work parties. At Tacloban, I volunteered to be a member of a work party.

The land portion of the Red Beach supply depot was enclosed by barbed wire. Armed guards were stationed at intervals along the perimeter. There were several openings in the barbed wire for vehicles. The best way to get out of the area was as a passenger on one of the trucks.

Some of the soldiers told us that there was a village two miles down the road. Burvel Dean Weaver, a fellow cooks-striker from Cameron, Missouri was on the work party with me. Weaver and I brought a couple of cartons of cigarettes ashore with us in case we got a chance to go to town. I asked him if he wanted to go to the village. He said sure. We checked with our shipmates on the work party with us to see if it was okay. They said to go ahead; they would cover for us.

We asked an Army truck driver if we could catch a ride to the village down the road. He said, "Sure, soon as we're loaded, hop aboard." Both the driver and the soldier in the cab with him were armed with carbines. They told us there were still Japanese soldiers in the jungle that did not know that the war was suppose to be over, but the area around the village should be all right. With our cartons of cigarettes in hand, we climbed into the back of the truck. Squeezing into an open area among the boxes of cargo, off we went on our Tacloban adventure.

As we were leaving the guarded beach compound, we joined a small convoy of trucks that were taking food and ammunition to one of our infantry bases in the mountains. Our soldiers were daily going out on patrols to find Japanese stragglers who were still in the jungle and didn't know that the war was over.

Along the way, our driver started talking to his buddy and forgot all about us until he was about ten miles away from the beach. Weaver and I were sitting in the canvas covered cargo area, talking and enjoying our ride through the jungle, not realizing that we had passed our destination and were moving quite a distance away from Red Beach. Gradually the two-lane Army Corps of Engineers road was narrowing to become a one-lane, enlarged jungle trail just wide enough for two vehicles to squeeze by each other.

Our truck stopped. The driver came back and apologized to us. He had forgotten that we were back in the cargo area and had driven right past the turnoff to the village. He said we should be all right. The front of the convoy were unloading their supplies and would soon be returning along this road back to the beach for another load. We said okay, then climbed out of the truck and started walking down the road toward Red Beach.

There we were, two sailors, each armed with a carton of cigarettes, walking along a darkening jungle road on an island containing hostile Japanese soldiers who were unaware the war was over.

Leyte is about ten degrees north of the Equator. At this latitude, every day of the year has basically twelve hours of daylight and twelve hours of darkness. The nighttime curtain of darkness falls rapidly. Even the light from a full moon is partially blocked by the canopy of jungle growth.

After darkness fell, we really became concerned. Walking down the road, we could hear our footsteps; otherwise it was quiet except for some occasional eerie sounds that came from the vegetation along the roadside. Then from the road behind us, we heard the familiar sound of an engine. As the sound grew louder, through the darkness, we saw two narrow slits of light that looked like glowing cat's eyes slowly moving toward us. Soon, the outline of a truck appeared.

Weaver and I moved into the center of the road and began waving our arms to attract attention. As the truck came closer to us, we could see that the glow of lights from the vehicle was from the narrow openings in the metal blackout covers over the headlights.

The driver saw us standing in the roadway and cautiously slowed the truck to a stop. The armed soldier on the passenger side of the cab pointed his rifle at us and gruffly asked, "Who are you? What are you doing up here in the hills?"

We told him we were sailors from one of the ships in the harbor and were going to the village. He said, "You sailors, don't you know there are still Jap soldiers around here? Get in the back of the truck!"

They took us to Red Beach where we rejoined our work party. Our buddies did a great job covering for us. We were not missed. We owed them one. It was a scary experience.

SUNDAY, SEPTEMBER 16, 1945
TACLOBAN, SAN PEDRO BAY, LEYTE, PHILIPPINE ISLANDS

Since we were still under partial wartime conditions, no one was officially allowed ashore for recreational purposes. Even though it was against naval regulations, to help relieve the tension beginning to build up among the crew, the captain announced after supper that we could each have a ration of two cans of beer.

Cases of warm beer were brought to the scullery where I helped serve them to the crew. They didn't seem to care that the beer was warm. This was a rare treat, which the crew appreciated. At times, the captain could be a nice guy. He seemed to understand the pressures the crew was under due to the stress of prolonged sea duty under hazardous conditions.

Now that the war was supposed to be over and we didn't have to darken the ship, a large canvas movie screen was rigged on the mast adjacent to the aft hatch. We were able to watch movies topside in the comfort of our own tropical, open-air theater.

That night the movie was The Adventures of Robin Hood with Earl Flynn, Olivia DeHavilland and Basil Rathbone. I think it was the third time we had seen it. At least Robin Hood was a lot better than some of the old Saturday-afternoon Grade B flicks that we had seen.

During the movies, the officers sat on chairs on the officers' country area of the superstructure, which overlooked the aft hatch. The enlisted men sat on the hatch covers and the surrounding main deck.

Naval tradition says that the movie does not start until the captain and his party has arrived and is seated. When the film is over, naval tradition again says no one can leave until after the captain and his party has departed.

The captain was a nice guy, but we thought sometimes he might have had too many cocktails. On more than one occasion he would look a little unsteady when he arrived to take his seat. After the movie was over, we would turn to see if he had left or was leaving so that we could go. Many times, our beloved leader would be sound asleep. One of the officers sitting next to him would have to wake him up so that the crew could leave.

MONDAY, SEPTEMBER 17, 1945, RED BEACH TACLOBAN, SAN PEDRO BAY, LEYTE, PHILIPPINE ISLANDS

Today we had two members of our crew returned to the ship under armed guard. Boatswain Caro and Coxswain Norbert Franxman were not aboard the *Fergus* when we left Manila. No one knew what had happened to them.

With the compliments of the United States Army Air Corps, they were flown to Leyte from Luzon where they had turned themselves in for being AWOL and Missing Ship.

Those offenses are very serious and could mean years in a naval prison. Boatswain Caro and Franxman both had exemplary war records.

The bos'n had almost three-and-one-half years of continual sea duty. During that period of time, he received one thirty-day leave between his last ship and the *Fergus*. Caro had pre-war duty in the Philippines and had friends in Manila. This was his first time back to the city since the war started.

When he went ashore, he looked up some Filipino friends to see if they had survived the conflict. He found them and they celebrated their own personal VJ Day. He got lost in Manila.

Franxman had been aboard our ship since last spring. Prior to joining the crew of the *Fergus*, he had over two years of sea duty aboard the battleship USS *Colorado* (BB 45) where he participated in seven major naval campaigns.

Franxman was a coxswain of a LCVP boat. The day before we sailed from Manila, he made a liberty run to the fleet landing. He told his crew to take a break. Then, he cast off the lines and took off with the boat. Not knowing where he was going or when he would be back, his crew made their way back to our ship on another LCVP. After almost three continuous years of sea duty with only one thirty days leave, the coxswain decided that he needed a vacation. He took his boat up the Pasig River and went on a holiday in Manila.

Upon being returned to our ship, Franxman went to the brig and the bos'n was confined to his quarters. Later, because the bos'n was a highly respected chief warrant officer and a key member of the ship's company, the captain chastised him and put him on liberty restriction for an indefinite period of time.

Franxman was different. He was a lower ranking petty officer and he had taken one of our LCVP Boats. If he had just gone AWOL, that would have been just one thing, but being AWOL and taking government property made the offenses very serious.

Because of the coxswain's commendable war record and his years of continuous sea duty, the captain offered him an unusual, yet very fair, sentence. He had a choice:

A General Court Martial with the possibility of a few years in a naval prison and upon completion of his sentence he would receive a Dishonorable or Bad Conduct Discharge

Or the following (which is the sentence he wisely chose):

"Demotion to Seaman Second Class (one rank above a recruit); serve thirty days confinement in the brig on bread and water with a full meal every third day."

Then, after serving his brig time:

Every day until we arrived back in the States, for one hour, from 12 noon to 1300, he was to march with a military bearing around the outside walkway of the superstructure near the quarterdeck.

While doing his punishment parade, he was to:

1. Wear the dress uniform for the area (in the tropics it was whites).
2. His hat was to be squared.
3. Wear a backpack containing fifty pounds of anchor chain.
4. Have an unloaded rifle on his shoulder.

The captain said, "Regardless of the weather, he is going to do his

Norb Franxman, 1945, walking off his punishment for his "holiday" in Manila.

punishment time walking across the Pacific," and he did. So much for his holiday in Manila.

Before his vacation in Manila, I knew Franxman as a shipmate, but not a friend. He was the coxswain whose quick reactions at Ulithi saved my head from being crushed when I fell into the water between the two boats. After he was busted to Seaman Second class, they sent him to work as a mess-cook in the galley.

We worked together for several months and became friends. After returning to civilian life, we exchanged Christmas cards and letters. In the 1960's, he moved to California with his wife and children. We remained close friends until he recently passed away.

The same day that Bos'n Caro and Franxman were returned to the ship, we received aboard ship 630 soldiers from the 9th Army Corps. Our passengers were one officer and five enlisted men of the Food Veterinary Inspection team, two officers and 118 enlisted men from the 306th Engineers and members of the 37th Field Hospital. The other troops were members of the 321st Infantry and various other Army combat units.

Along with the soldiers, we received barges filled with crates and various types of mechanical equipment. Everything they brought to us was loaded aboard. Items were stored in every possible spot on deck and in the cargo holds. There wasn't much room to move around on the ship. This was the most men and equipment we had ever carried.

Several crates of our cargo were classified as secret. They were clustered together and marine guards were posted around the area. We were ordered to stay away.

CHAPTER IX

CONVOY TO OCCUPY AOMORI, NORTHERN HONSHU, JAPAN

TUESDAY, SEPTEMBER 18, 1945
AT SEA

We left Leyte in a thirty-ship convoy heading to Aomori, Northern Honshu, Japan. Rear Admiral Richard L. Conolly, USN on the USS *Appalachian* (AGC 1, ComPhibGroup 3) was the commander of our convoy. We were: Transport Division 44 of Task Group 34 of Plan A-304-45.

Admiral Conolly had a reputation of being an aggressive leader. His nickname was "Close-In Conolly." He received the name when he was in charge of the operation to capture the islands of Roi-Namur in the Marshall Islands.

Having been at the invasion of Tarawa Atoll, he recognized the mistakes that had been made during the pre-invasion bombardments to "soften up" Betio island. In the Marshall Islands, he insisted that the warships under his command move "close in" to the beaches. There, they hit the enemy, with a prolonged maximum-effort pre-invasion bombardment. Once our troops were on the beaches, his ships remained at their "close in " positions to provide additional support fire when and where needed. The admiral's tactics were a strong factor in our forces suffering minimal casualties as they quickly accomplished their objective.

Our convoy formed into cruising disposition 2T, with intervals of 1,000 yards, distances of 600 yards. The USS *Kershaw* (APA 176) was the guide. The standard speed was fourteen knots. The *Fergus* was the fourth ship in the third column, Division A, Trans Div 44.

We were also joined by the USS *Rockingham* (APA 229), the USS *Shoshone* (AKA 65), the USS *Berrien* (APA 62), the USS *Catron* (APA 71) and the USS *Crittenden* (APA 77). The *Berrien*, *Catron* and *Crittenden* were twin-stacker sister ships to the *Fergus*.

We went back under wartime conditions, with darkened ship at night. General Quarters was sounded and we conducted anti-aircraft practice. The war might have been over, but we were not taking any chances.

WEDNESDAY, 19 SEPTEMBER 1945. AT SEA

We had an incident this morning, which could have really been nasty. One of our boatswain's mates, was master-at-arms. At reveille—the time we are supposed to get up in the morning—the master-at-arms walks around the ship, switching on the lights in the various compartments and sometimes hitting the bunks with his nightstick to make sure everyone is awake.

Our infantrymen passengers had been living under primitive conditions for almost a year. You could see the apprehensive wariness of combat-hardened riflemen in their eyes. The strong musty odor of the tropical rain forests had permeated into their clothes and even into the pores of their skin. They smelled like the jungle.

As soldiers in the Philippine Islands, they had spent months in the soggy humid jungle where they could never really relax. With their rifles always at their side, their nights were frequently spent half-asleep and half-awake as they tried to get some rest.

The sounds of the jungle with its dangers from snakes, spiders and other predatory animals, compounded by the threat of nighttime infiltration or counter-attack by Japanese soldiers, were with them every day.

One of the favorite tactics of the Japanese soldiers was to creep up on our troops in the darkness of the night while they were sleeping or dozing in their foxholes or forward bivouac areas and slit their throats. For infantrymen, the dangers were constant. Survival was based on constant vigilance and minimal-to-no mistakes.

Many of our passengers had landed in the Philippines with MacArthur the previous September. Even though the troop quarters were crowded with bunks stacked four to six tiers high, most of the soldiers seemed to appreciate being dry and having clean bunks. There were not many complaints. The previous night was the first time in almost a year that most of them had a safe and sound night's sleep.

At 0530 (5:30 a.m.), the master-at-arms went into the aft troop-berthing quarters. He turned on the light and began hitting the bunks with his nightstick and yelling "Reveille, reveille! Drop your cocks and grab your socks." He did the wrong thing.

Four of the soldiers rolled out of their bunks, grabbed the master-at-arms, took his night stick away, and picked him up as he started shouting, squirming and kicking. They carried him topside. Along the way, he created quite a commotion. By the time the soldiers got him out on deck, the on-duty personnel of the ship's company in the area could hear that something was happening.

We had armed Marine guards stationed throughout the ship, especially in the areas of the troop quarters. The noise alerted the Marines. Their lieutenant, along with two of the Marines, rushed toward the commotion just as the soldiers were lifting the master-at-arms up to the rail. They were about to throw him over the side. The Marine Lieutenant shouted, "Halt! Put that man down!"

The four soldiers stopped and turned to see our Marine Lieutenant with a cocked forty-five caliber pistol in his hand, and the other two Marines with their carbines pointed at them. Slowly, they lowered the shaken master-at-arms down to the deck and put their hands up. The Marines promptly placed the soldiers under arrest. The master-at-arms was fortunate. He could have ended up trying to swim in shark-infested tropical waters.

Those jungle fighters had a short fuse. Future wake-up calls were made with much less vigor. I don't know what happened to the soldiers. For the rest of the time that they were aboard our ship, they were confined to the brig on bread and water. After we reached Japan, they went ashore with the rest of the troops and the Army handled any further disciplinary action.

With the war supposedly over, the crew was more relaxed. After we left Leyte, I heard of another incident that could have been awkward.

MIDNIGHT STOREROOM (APRICOTED-OUT)

Al Herrington and some of his Texas buddies were part of the work party that helped load supplies in the aft number two hold.

To sailors, food was an important item. They always seemed to keep their eyes open for an opportunity to set aside some goodies for a "hungry day." When you were a growing seventeen-eighteen year old, every day seemed to be a hungry day.

The basic rule for loading the ship was to put items aboard in sequential order. The first to be unloaded would be the last to be loaded or "last on, first off." The less important items were placed in the lower levels of the cargo hold. Usually shipments of food were assigned to a special cargo area using the same offloading priority system.

The sailors knew that they had stacked cases of canned apricots and fruit cocktail in a corner of the number two hold. What they did not know was that several cases of ammunition were also stacked in the same area.

Wherever ammunition was stored, our ship's policy was to have armed-marine -guards stationed in the area twenty-four hours a day. Otherwise for shipboard security, especially when we had troops aboard, the guards would be strategically located throughout the ship.

The cargo holds had air vents, which were pipes running from the storage areas up to the deck of the ship. Several of the air vents were a fairly good size. With some effort a thin or small person could fit in one.

One evening, Herrington and four of his buddies were hungry. They decided to liberate a case of apricots from the "midnight storeroom" in the number two hold. An air vent that was located out of the direct sight of the marine guard would be the best place to send the thinnest guy down the vent for the food. That sailor was Charles Benton, from Broken Bow, Oklahoma. They tied a line around him and he was quietly lowered through the opening into the storage area.

Benton made it down without any problems. Groping around in the semi-darkness, he located a wooden box he thought contained canned apricots. He moved the box over to the area under the air duct, tied a line around it and gave the signal for his shipmates above to hoist away. With the surging and rolling motions of the ship, the wooden container was carefully liberated. The sounds of the engines and the seawater against the hull of the ship helped to muffle any sounds the box made on its journey out of the hold.

When they finally got the box on deck, much to their surprise, the apricots turned out to be a case of hand grenades. They quickly lowered the grenades back down the vent along with a note that Benton could barely read in the semi-darkness. The note informed him what was in the box, and to read the label before sending anything else up.

Finally he found a case of apricots and sent it up to his buddies. Later, Herrington told me that they had eaten so much of it that whenever apricots were being served in the chow line, they passed it by. They were apricoted-out.

MONDAY, 24 SEPTEMBER 1945. AT SEA

As we proceeded northward from Leyte toward Japan, from islands along the way, ships converged on us. By the time we were off the coast of Northern Honshu, our convoy had grown to be almost 100 ships. We were a sizable task force.

This was quite an operation, especially when you realized that we were just one segment of the fleet of ships and the tens to hundreds of thousands of troops that were converging upon and landing at strategically located areas of the Japanese homeland.

At 0800 (8 a.m.) we sighted Honshu, the main island of Japan. Steaming in the same formation, our speed was reduced to eight knots because we were approaching a minefield.

With Japanese charts to guide us, prior to reaching the minefield, the convoy assumed an inverted V formation. Wooden-hulled minesweepers took the point of the formation. These small ships were a little larger than the fishing boats that were common along the coast of California. The reason why they were made of wood was to protect them from magnetic mines that would be drawn to steel hulled ships.

With the USS *Kershaw* (APA 176) as the convoy guide, we maintained our assigned position as the fourth ship in the third column. At 1645 (2:45 p.m.) we went into Mine Cruising Disposition 2 T and commenced steaming our paravanes, which means we put them into the water and trolled them on either side of the ship.

Paravanes are small airplane shaped water kites, which were attached to specially designed three-strand wire rope. These water kites were used to locate and cut the mooring cables of submerged mines and bring (or pop) them to the surface. One of our paravanes on its sweeping path through the water popped a mine.

Using a Springfield rifle, one of our gunner's mates fired five shots at the bobbing target. His fifth shot hit a spike on the mine and exploded it. He was quite a marksman. I shudder to think what it would have been like trying to go through those hazardous waters without the Japanese charts to help guide us.

TUESDAY, 25 SEPTEMBER 1945 (MONTH TWELVE) AOMORI BAY, NORTHERN HONSHU, JAPAN

We arrived off the coast of the northern tip of Honshu, near the entrance to Aomori Bay last night. Our convoy consisted of three heavy cruisers, two carriers, twenty-three destroyers, eleven destroyer escorts, twenty-nine attack transports (APAs) with combat infantrymen and their support personnel, five attack cargo transports (AKAs) with combat troops and their cargo plus twenty LCIs (Landing Craft Infantry, which are small sea going ships that were used primarily to carry personnel and land them directly onto hostile beaches).

With well over 20,000 seasoned combat troops and their equipment, we were a formidable group. Our guns were loaded with live ammunition; we were manned and ready for whatever resistance that may be facing us. The aircraft carriers stood offshore. Their airplanes provided protective air cover for us against any potential Kamikaze air attacks or hostile shore fire.

A few days before our arrival in Northern Honshu, an advance party had landed at Aomori. They talked to the local officials and received navigational charts plus the locations of the minefields in the area. Also, S. Nakamura a Japanese Naval Officer accompanied by LTJG R. Boggess, USNR, a linguist who spoke fluent Japanese, were flown to one of our carriers. They were then taken to Admiral Connoly's Command ship. The day before we were scheduled to enter Aomori Bay, Nakamura and Boggess were transferred along with copies of the charts to one of the minesweepers. The minesweepers were the small wooden-hulled boats that were out in front clearing the passageway for our invasion occupation force.

As the sun began to rise above the mountains surrounding the bay, the shallow-draft vessels —with the Japanese pilot and our linguist on the lead ship—led the convoy into the bay through the pathway that was cleared in the minefields.

Then came the cruisers, destroyers and destroyer escorts with their heavy firepower. "In Close Connoly" lived up to his reputation; he placed his warships in the forefront. Once inside the bay, they fanned out to form a protective shield for the troop transports.

With our paravanes out, we went into Cruising Disposition 4 T. After we were safely inside the bay, we retrieved our paravanes and went to our assigned location. The captain then set Condition One Able (all personnel aboard ship were to report to their assigned combat landing stations). My One Able station was as ammunition handler for a 20-mm gun on the superstructure above the bridge. I had an unobstructed view of the entire operation.

From his command ship, Admiral Connoly issued the order to commence the operation. The captain relayed the orders for us to put our boats into the water. At the same time the other APAs and AKAs were launching their boats. We then began debarking our troops and cargo. The term D-Day refers to the Debarkation Day when troops are off-loaded from the ships and taken ashore. Every combat landing has a D-Day.

After the LCVP boats from the APAs and AKAs were in the water and loaded with their passengers or cargo, they formed circling formations near their mother ships. When the signal was given from the command ship for the boats to "Land Your Troops," the first wave of the LCI's and LCVP boats started moving toward the beach at flank speed. It was exciting to watch. We really put on a show as we accomplished our mission of landing occupation forces and their equipment in and around Aomori, Northern Honshu, Japan. The landing was a powerful demonstration of America's might and precision.

SEABEES

When the first wave of our landing crafts returned to the ship, the boat crews said that Seabees had put up a big sign on a waterfront dock saying, "Welcome to Japan." Which meant that they had been there several days before and had swept the area for any mines or other hazards to our ships.

The Seabees (CBs) were, and still are, the Navy's Construction Battalion, similar to the Army Corps of Engineers. They were the sailors/builders whose responsibility was to clear mines and any obstacles from invasion landing areas, and then landed on those hostile beaches with their bulldozers and construction equipment.

Once ashore, many times, in the midst of the battle, they went about their business of constructing airfields, roads and anything else needed to accomplish the mission of invading and occupying enemy territory.

They were usually older men (18 to 50, with a reported average age of 37) who had been in the construction business before the war. They didn't get much publicity like the Marines or the Frogmen (Underwater Demolition Teams).

The Seabees deserve more credit than they have received. Without their courage and construction skills, our island-hopping campaign would have been much more prolonged and difficult than it was. Their motto is "Can Do," and they have certainly more than lived up to their creed.

WEDNESDAY, 26 SEPTEMBER 1945
AOMORI, NORTHERN HONSHU, JAPAN

Two US Naval officers and a Japanese pilot came aboard our ship. Lt J.M. Algeo, USN, a pilot and the linguist, Lt. Boggess, accompanied J. Hakashima, a Japanese Naval Officer who acted as our pilot. Hakashima took over the con under the supervision of Lts. Alego and Boggess and navigated the ship to the port city of Aomori Ko.

Without any tugboats to help, we were able to tie up to the starboard side of pier # 1. Sure enough, there was the sign, WELCOME TO JAPAN. The rest of that day and night we completed unloading our troops and cargo.

They said that fifty-seven Americans were being held as prisoners-of-war in a near-by Japanese labor camp. The POW's would either come aboard our ship, one of the other APAs, for medical treatment or be flown by the Army Air Corps to Guam. They were reported to be in very poor physical condition.

As we were pulling into the port area, we got our first real look at Aomori. The city, according to the 1940 census, was supposed to have a population of 99,000 people. Considering that it had such a large population, there were only a few hundred people in town and very few structures were left standing.

The captain said that we had come a long way to get here. Even though it was not authorized, he was going to allow each member of our ship's company to go ashore so that we could say that we had landed on and occupied Japan. We were required to stay together and follow directions. In small, unarmed groups we went ashore and—in formation—walked around the city.

Our tour guide was a US Navy Petty Officer. He informed us that

September 1945. Aamori, Northern Honshu, Japan. Top three photos are bomb destroyed buildings in the city, bottom photo shows the docking area for ships.

Aomori was an industrial city whose buildings were primarily constructed with wood. Several weeks before we arrived, our aircraft had devastated the area with firebombs. The bombing raids reportedly created a firestorm, which almost completely destroyed every wooden structure in the city.

The industriousness of the Japanese was demonstrated in this community. Less than a month after the cessation of hostilities, most of the debris from the bombing raids had been cleared away. We were surprised that they were already starting to rebuild the main part of the town.

On our walking tour, we passed some strange looking small-concrete-block-type structures and several small newly constructed wooden buildings. There must have been a shortage of metal for nails because a rope-like twine held together the walls of the wooden buildings. The twine was similar to the material that they used to make their hats. There were three automobiles parked along the side of the roadway. One was a tiny vehicle that was made in Japan. The other two were from America. One of the American cars was a 1935 Buick that had a charcoal burner attached to it for its source of power.

The civilians in town were either old men or young kids. Many of them were dressed in shabby-looking uniform type clothing with wraparound puttee-leggings similar to those the American soldiers wore during World War I. We did not see any women, babies or Japanese military.

On the waterfront docks, small groups of older men were clustered together in squat sitting positions. Stoically they stared at us and our ship. I did not feel comfortable at the way they looked at us.

Most of the population—including the women—must have moved out of the city up into the mountains. Some of the boat crews said that they had seen some older women and some young children in the small fishing villages that dotted the perimeter of the bay.

RUSSIANS WERE STOPPED

The primary mission of our task force was to land troops and occupy this portion of northern Honshu, Japan. Once our military personnel were strategically entrenched in various locations around Aomori, Admiral Conolly ordered the carriers and cruisers back to sea. The secondary phase of their mission was a move in the world game of "political chess."

Under combat alert conditions, they sailed through the Tsugaru Strait between Aomori, Northern Honshu, and Hakodate, Southern Hokkaido, into the Sea of Japan. Their job was to discourage and—if necessary— stop the Russians from attempting to occupy the strategically located northern islands of the Japanese homeland.

Later we heard that Russia had a non-aggression pact with the Japanese. On August 8, 1945—two days after the first atomic bomb was dropped on Hiroshima, Russia declared war against a weakened Japan that was facing imminent invasion by Allied forces.

On August 8, 1945, Joseph Stalin, the dictatorial ruler of the Soviet Union, demonstrated what a devious opportunist he was. On that date Stalin broke his non-aggression pact with Japan when he sent his troops across the Russia/China border to attack and invade Manchuria.

His aggressive strategy was to have Soviet forces occupy Northern China, Manchuria, Korea and as many of the islands of the Japanese homeland as they could. The Russian struck so swiftly and decisively in Manchuria and Korea that they overwhelmed the Japanese troops and took over 1,200,000 of them as prisoners.

We also learned that Stalin had amassed 50,000 Russian soldiers in the eastern portion of the Soviet Union. He had plans underway for those troops to invade and occupy Hokkaido, the northernmost of the major Japanese homeland islands.

The presence of our troops in Aomori and at other key strategic locations plus our impressive naval task force was a show of strength to emphasize to the Russians that we were occupying the northern islands of Japan. At the time we didn't realize that this standoff with the Soviets was one of the initial phases in the onset of the ensuing decades-long Cold War conflict between the Soviet Bloc and the Western Nations.

SATURDAY, 29 SEPTEMBER 1945

We departed Aomori, Japan, in a convoy of ten ships under the command of Commodore Popham, COM TRANS RON 15, task Group 34.3 aboard the USS *Bayfield*, (APA 33). The *Fergus* was the fourth ship in the left column. Our standard speed was 15 knots. The USS *Culvert M. Moore* (DE 442) was one of our escorts. They said we were going to Tokyo, to pick up POW's and then go home. Later the same day we learned that we were actually going to Saipan in the Mariana Islands.

CHAPTER X

A TYPHOON AT SAIPAN
AND HOMEWARD BOUND

5 OCTOBER 1945. SAIPAN, MARIANA ISLANDS

During the night, we went through a typhoon. I never want to have that experience again. We were anchored on the western (lee) side of the island. The weather seemed normal throughout the day and into the early evening. Then the winds began to increase in intensity and the seas started getting heavy, but that was not too unusual.

Around 2000 (8 p.m.) there was a dramatic change in the weather. At 2230 (10:30 p.m.) the Special Sea Detail was set. The intensity of the elements developed into one of the most violent typhoons to hit that area in decades.

In the fierceness of the full force of the storm, the winds were so strong that you could not be out in the elements or you would be blown overboard. The rain was so heavy that, from the bridge, I couldn't see our bow.

We had merchant ships anchored behind us and Navy ships in front and to the sides of us. There were so many vessels surrounding us, we couldn't get underway. The Navy had radar, but some of the merchant ships didn't.

With so many ships around us, we had to maintain our mooring position. Consequently, we deployed an additional anchor so that we had two of them out, one on the port and one on the starboard side of the bow. At the height of the storm when the wind, rain, and sea were at their strongest, we had both anchors out and our engines were running at their flank speed, which drove our two propellers to their maximum turning capacity. Still we had difficulty maintaining our position. At times we were dangerously dragging the anchors. It was difficult to keep from colliding with the other ships around us. Under those hazardous conditions, we remained at our Special Sea Detail stations for over twelve hours.

Fortunately, we weathered the storm without colliding with any of the other vessels or sustaining any serious damage to our ship. It was a long night and morning.

Later in the day, after the storm had passed, we learned that a seaman from one of the freighters had been washed overboard into the boiling seas. By some miraculous stroke of fate, a wave lifted him out of the water and tossed him onto the deck of an adjacent ship. To the amazement of the crew of that vessel, they saw an unknown person floundering around on the deck of their ship.

A merchant seaman volunteered to attempt to rescue him. The seaman—with a line tied round his waist that was tended by some of his shipmates went out into the raging storm. On deck, he worked his way over to the person, grasped the Kapok life jacket he was wearing and dragged him to the safety of the enclosed portion of the ship. The Kapok life jacket undoubtedly helped to save the waterlogged sailor's life.

Later, we heard that this storm continued building in intensity as it moved westward. When it hit Okinawa, ships at anchor on the windward side of the island were tossed up onto the beaches like they were matchsticks. It was reported to be one of the most destructive typhoons to hit that region in recent history.

I had never seen nor could have imagined the rage of the boiling sea and the powerful destructiveness winds. They said that we were within ten miles from the peak of the intensity of the storm. At 1800 (6 p.m.) we got underway for Guam.

SATURDAY, 6 OCTOBER 1945
GUAM, MARIANA ISLANDS

We arrived in Guam at 0900. We received mail, our first in over a month. There were five letters from my folks. My mom was certainly wonderful about writing. She would tell me about our family, the local news and my dog "Boots." Without her letters, mail call would have been a real disappointment. I tried to write home as often as I could.

The nice part about mail call was hearing about what was happening back home. The sad part was not receiving a letter from a loved one. Some of the men didn't get any mail at all. It must have been tough. They looked lonely and lost.

The toughest part about being at sea was the lack of communication. Sometimes there would be two to three months between mail deliveries. I wished that my girlfriend from high school would write. I hadn't received anything from her in over six months. She must have been busy. With all of the dances and proms, she was probably going out with someone else. I couldn't blame her.

It was certainly better to not receive letters from a former girlfriend, than not to hear from your wife. One of the fellows I knew kept looking for a letter from his wife. She had not written in a long time. Now there was a guy with problems.

Many of the old-time sailors, seldom if ever, received any letters. The Navy was their family, and their home was the ship and the sea. Maybe that was why—when they went ashore on liberty—some of them drank too much, fought and just generally created havoc wherever they went. At sea they were the nicest guys in the world, but ashore you wanted to stay away from them.

Boatswain Caro was an interesting person. He was a leader that knew our ship and the sea. As a chief warrant officer, he lived in the officer's quarters, but did not seem to associate with them. He pretty much kept to himself. During the months that I was on our ship, he only seemed to be friendly with Chief Gunners Mate Edwards and a couple of the other chiefs.

The crew respected him yet, we were curious, no one ever heard him talk about his personal life. He seemed to be a man of mystery. We wondered if he had any family. Someone said that he listed a stepmother living in Long Beach, California as his next of kin. Like many of the old-time sailors, the Navy seemed to be his family and the ship was his home.

A sailor's life can be a lonely life. You could be surrounded by a thousand men and still be alone. Thank goodness the war was over and we were going home.

SUNDAY, OCTOBER 7, 1945. AT SEA
EN ROUTE FROM GUAM TO SAN FRANCISCO

We had more passengers aboard than we had ever thought we could carry (1004 enlisted men, 39 officers). They were Navy personnel eligible for discharge because they had more than enough points. Some of them had been out of the States for two to three years.

Throughout the ship hammocks strung up and cots were placed in almost every area that did not impede the flow of traffic. Our compartment was still too stuffy and hot for me to get a good night's sleep. Weather permitting, I went topside and slept in my hammock. There, I would be rocked to sleep by the rolling motion of the *Fergus* as she carried us to California. This voyage was truly a Sentimental Journey. We were homeward bound.

MONDAY, 8 OCTOBER 1945. AT SEA

High school English and Math classes started for members of the crew that didn't have their high school diplomas. There were quite a few of us aboard ship who had left school in our junior or senior years. Some of the older members of the crew had only completed the eighth grade. This was not uncommon for young people during the economic depression years of the 1930's.

Lieutenant Cummins and Lieutenant Tipton were former college professors. With the captain's permission and guidance, they set up a course of study to help us obtain our high school diplomas. Mr. Cummins' classes were in high school-level English with an emphasis on grammar, vocabulary development and pronunciation. Mr. Tipton taught the fundamentals of math, commencing with simple eighth-grade arithmetic and progressing through algebra.

They recommended that all members of the crew that did not have their high school diploma should take these classes. Upon completion of the course of study, they would arrange for us to take an examination called the GED (General Educational Development) test. They said that we would receive our high school diploma if we received a passing score on the test.

I didn't understand it. All I had to do was take the classes and pass the GED test in order to receive my diploma. I had left school when I was in the first part of my junior year. I still had over a year and a half to go before I would be eligible to graduate. The thought of going back to San Jose High School and sitting in classrooms with all of those young kids wasn't too appealing.

Mr. Tipton and Mr. Cummins encouraged us to get our high school diplomas, and to go to college when we got out of the Navy. They told us that Congress had passed legislation called the GI Bill that would help us pay for our tuition and give us a monthly subsistence allowance while we were in school. First, I had to get my high school diploma. I took the classes and later the GED test.

THURSDAY, 11 OCTOBER 1945. AT SEA
NORTHWEST OF MIDWAY ISLAND
FIRE IN THE FORWARD HOLD

Even though the war was over, the captain still had us conducting emergency drills. We continued to have GQ along with various other drills, such as Fire and Damage Control.

The fire drill became a reality to the crew of the *Fergus* on three occasions. One was a report of smoke emanating from the aft 20-mm ammunition-handling room, which fortunately proved to be a minor electrical malfunction. The other was an arson fire that was set in a washroom used by the troops. The third was cargo in the forward hold while we were at sea, northeast of the Hawaiian Islands.

For some unknown reason, the cargo started smoldering, and broke into flames. The alarm was sounded and we all went to our fire stations. As recruits in the Navy, we went through damage-control school and were trained to be firefighters.

Upon reporting aboard ship, one of my collateral assignments was as a member of a damage control fire-fighting team. My duty was to be a line-handler for the fireman who went into the area of smoke or flames to extinguish the fire. When the alarm sounded and the dreaded words, "Fire in the number one hold, this is no drill," came over the ship's PA system, we quickly went to our fire stations. My duty station was near the location of the fire.

Our damage control officer, Lieutenant F. J. Weiss from San Francisco, California, checked the manifest of the cargo in the hold. He said the area primarily contained canvas sacks of mail that we had loaded aboard at Guam. Thank goodness we didn't have ammunition or highly flammable items near the fire.

My firefighter received the assignment of being the first into the hold. His task was to assess the situation and, if possible, put out the fire. My job as his line tender was to make sure that his lifeline was free and clear. If he got into trouble, it was my responsibility to pull him out or, if necessary, go in and get him out.

The rest of the firefighting team helped to control and feed the heavy fire hose. When everyone was in place, the hose man stepped from the passageway into the smoke-filled hatchway and began to spray water into the forward hold.

With a few minutes of maximum water volume from our hose, the smoke began to subside. Eventually, after a prolonged soaking, the smoldering fire was finally extinguished. The residue of the damaged mail sacks were removed from the area and taken topside by other members of our firefighting team.

It was unfortunate that the fire had to be in the mail sacks. There were quite a few families back in the States who would not be receiving letters from their loved ones. At sea, a fire aboard ship is one of the more feared dangers. Thank goodness we caught it before it spread.

SATURDAY, 20 OCTOBER 1945
SAN FRANCISCO AND HOME

As we approached the Golden Gate Bridge, we could see big signs hanging from it saying "Welcome Home" and "Well Done." People were standing on the bridge waving. Some of them tossed flowers to us from the railings. It was a memorable emotional experience.

On the San Francisco side of the bridge were fireboats spraying giant plumes of water. They were our escorts as we moved into the beautiful San Francisco Bay. It was nice to be back in the States. We tied up to Pier 7, and began disembarking our passengers.

From San Francisco, we went to Mare Island Naval Shipyard for repairs. We were less than one hundred miles away from San Jose and my home. But, since we were only going to be in port for a short period of time, all personnel were needed to help get the *Fergus* ready for sea. Therefore, we were only allowed liberty every other day and we had to be back aboard ship by sundown. All I could do was make a few telephone

Golden West Cafe, Georgia St., Vallejo. October 1945. Just returned to the "States;" we were all 18-19 years old. Left to right: Braun, Weaver, Cheeves, Norman, Beadle, and Reding.

calls to my folks. I tried to reach my girlfriend, but she was not at home.

At that time Mare Island had a naval hospital, which took care of amputees. When we were tied up to the dock, a young Marine with a leg missing came aboard our ship. He had been one of the troops we transported the first time we went to the war zone. A shell fragment from a mortar round hit him soon after he landed on Okinawa. The Marine remembered the name and number of our ship and wanted to come aboard to look around. He stopped by the galley because he had worked there as a mess-cook. I remembered him because he was about my age and we had worked together for almost a month.

I asked him what happened to his outfit after they left our ship. He said that they had suffered almost a hundred percent casualties—either killed or wounded. I wish I had written down his name. He was a nice guy; I hope he was able to adjust to civilian life.

Years later I was talking to the son-in-law of one of the other Marines that we transported from San Diego to Okinawa. The Marine's name was Private Glendon Collins. He was from Arkansas. Even though Collins was 29 years old, married and had two young daughters, in November 1944 he was drafted into the Marine Corps. He arrived on Okinawa in May 1945 and was killed in action on June 7th 1945. He is buried at the Punch Bowl National Cemetery on Oahu, in Hawaii.

CHAPTER XI

THE MAGIC CARPET

In preparation for the invasion of Japan, the United States and its Allies had assembled a huge armada of ships and several million troops and support personnel in Australia, New Zealand, China, Burma, India, the Philippines and the other islands of the central and western Pacific. This massive invasion force was projected to be the largest force of men, aircraft, ships and materials ever assembled in the history of warfare.

During the course of being involved in a worldwide conflict, the Allies had stationed military personnel in Europe, North Africa, the Pacific, Australia and Asia. With the combat portion of the war over, the allies were faced with the monumental logistical task of returning the millions of our service personnel back to their homes. To compound the problem was what to do with the defeated enemy's military personnel. After they were disarmed, arrangements were made to return them to their respective homelands.

One of America's challenges was: getting the millions of our men and women home for reassignment or to be returned to civilian status. In the Pacific Theater of Operations, this enormous logistical transportation task was called the Magic Carpet.

In 1945, there were very few aircraft capable of flying across the oceans of the world, especially the Pacific Ocean. Ships were the primary Trans-Atlantic or Trans-Pacific mode of transportation for almost all troops and cargo.

Top priority for the ride home was given to prisoners-of-war and the wounded that were able to travel. They received the finest treatment available on the first ships and trans-ocean type aircraft returning to the States.

Chief Gunner's Mate Edwards with the ship's mascot.

Jim Reding.

Left to right from back row: Gaide, Beatle, Schular, Reding. Front row: Putumann, Drake.

Our military personnel eligible for a discharge or for re-assignment were transported on every conceivable homeward bound vessel in the fleet from carriers to battleships and freighters. For subsequent shuttle trips, the task was primarily assigned to our converted passenger liners (AP's) and troop ships (APAs and AKAs).

SATURDAY, 3 NOVEMBER 1945

As an APA, the USS *Fergus* was assigned to the Magic Carpet. When our repairs were completed, we departed Mare Island and pulled alongside Pier 38 in San Francisco. Twenty-five officers and 326 men from the receiving ship on Treasure Island came aboard for transportation to Guam, Mariana Islands. They were replacement personnel.

We departed San Francisco for Guam and then we went on to Tacloban, Leyte, Philippine Islands, to pick up passengers and return them back to the States. This would be our second trip to Tacloban and our third to the western Pacific this year.

After a few days at sea, we were in the daily shipboard routine. With the war over, being young and restless, we were bored. To break the monotony, I dared a shipmate to get a short haircut. To my surprise, he said he would if I would. I said fine. I should have known better, the shipmate was Jerry Schular, from Everett, Washington. He was involved in the incident in San Diego where I was picked up by the shore patrol and thrown into the brig—while he got away.

Jerry had wavy red hair that was longer than most of the crew's. He was so proud of his hair. He would wear his hat on the back of his head with his wavy locks curling up in front of his white hat. We shook hands and went to the ship's barbershop. I was the first to sit down in the chair, and away went my hair. When the barber was almost through with my haircut, Schular took off.

Some of my buddies had heard about Schular taking off. They looked for him and he couldn't be found. That evening, he even skipped chow. Weaver, one of my friends, said, "Be patient—we'll get him tonight." Around midnight, when most of the crew was asleep, Weaver and I went to his compartment with two pairs of scissors. There he was, in his bunk, lying on his side, sound asleep.

In the subdued glow of the compartment's red night-lights, muffled by the sounds of the ship's engines and the seas against the ship's hull, we started clipping away at his prized locks of hair. We snipped away most of it on the left side of his head.

The next morning some of the fellows in his compartment said when Schular woke up he was livid. His face turned purple as he pounded his bunk shouting, "who did this"? Of course, no one knew anything about it, even though one of the sailors in his compartment had just gotten off watch and walked in as we were clipping away. No one said a word.

That morning, I was on duty in the galley. When he walked down the breakfast chow line, he had his wool watch cap pulled over his head down to his ears. He glared at me and said, "Reding, I'm going to get you!"

Later that morning, when the barbershop opened, he was the first one there to have his hair trimmed and balanced. Navy barbers didn't make appointments. But on that day, our barber told Schular his day was "filled with scheduled appointments" and he would have to come back tomorrow. Schular exploded with curses that would make a boatswain's mate blush.

For the rest of the day and that night, he wore his Navy blue wool watch-cap over his new hairdo. Smiling, members of the crew asked him why he was wearing his watch-cap. The following day he was back at the barbershop. Shaking his head with concern, the barber put Schular in the chair and said he would try to straighten out his midnight haircut.

When he got out of the chair, he looked like he was a new recruit in boot camp. He had received more of a shearing than a haircut. We all tried to help him learn that his word should be his word. Only time would tell if he learned his lesson. After a few days of being angry, he settled down and we were friends again.

PRISON OR SEA DUTY

The conclusion of hostilities and the downsizing of the forces result-ed in a shortage of skilled petty officers. This resulted in seasoned ship-board personnel being moved up to fill the empty slots. Consequently, there was a need for lower level enlisted personnel to do the so-called worker-bee jobs.

During the latter part of 1945 and the first part of 1946, with the cut-back in recruiting, personnel officers went to the naval prisons in order to fill those menial apprenticeship type jobs aboard our ships.

Prisoners with good attitudes who were facing one to two years of imprisonment and discharges which would be under less than under honorable conditions were given the opportunity to be released from prison. If they put in one year of sea duty—without any disciplinary incidents or any problems at all—when their one-year of sea duty was fulfilled, they would become eligible to receive a Discharge Under Honorable Conditions.

With a Bad Conduct or an Undesirable Discharge, there would be a blemish against their record for an indefinite period of time. A Discharge Under Honorable Conditions greatly reduced the negative stigma. Many of them wisely took advantage of the offer to go to sea for one year.

We received several of these men aboard our ship. Most of them were eighteen to twenty year olds who had gotten fouled up. They were all right, but we still had to watch them. A couple of them didn't last long. They were misfits who didn't seem to be meant for a life without bars in front of them. When an ex-prisoner didn't follow orders, at the next port he was quietly and quickly transferred off the ship. There were no third chances.

A sea-going sailor had to have the strength and flexibility to exercise good mental and physical discipline. If he could adjust to the regimented, monotonous and sometimes dangerous shipboard routine then sea duty could be fairly pleasant. If not, it could be an awful experience for the individual and everyone around him. To be confined in close quarters for a prolonged period of time takes a good-natured person, willing to follow orders and respect the rights and space of his shipmates. Sea duty is not for everyone.

MOONSHINE ON THE *FERGUS*

On our most recent trip to the Philippines we had an incident that almost sent a sailor back to prison. We had just transported replacement personnel from San Francisco to Tacloban. Prior to leaving San Francisco, we received seven new members to our ship's company. They were assigned to the deck force. Five of them were former inmates from a naval prison. They were being given a second chance.

If they got into any trouble, then they would be immediately returned to prison to complete their original sentences. They were pleasant, but you didn't want to get too close to them; they had problems. As deck hands, two of them were assigned to the galley as mess-cooks. I had one of them on my shift. He was lethargic and seemed to always to be looking for the easy way. You couldn't really rely on him.

After being underway for over a month, mostly in tropical waters, at 0231 (2:31 a.m.), we heard a loud explosion that sounded like we had been hit by a mine. The noise woke up everyone on the ship. From the Bridge, the officer of the deck immediately sounded the General Quarters alarm. By then we were so well trained that in three-and-a-half minutes we went from sound asleep in the middle of the night to having our battle stations manned and ready.

While we were manning our battle stations, the duty-officer-of-the-deck directed the damage control party to find out where the explosion occurred, what caused it and the extent of the damage to the ship.

After we had been at our battle stations for about fifteen minutes, we heard the familiar click which activated the ship's public address system. Without the customary sound of the boatswain's pipe or a calm voice giving us directions, the captain began to talk. You could feel the rage in his voice. He was furious.

When we had troops aboard, they would send some of their personnel to the galley as mess-cooks to help with the preparation and serving of meals. Also, we had members of the ship's company crew serve as mess-cooks. Someone had given one of the former prisoners, the recipe for brewing raisin-jack, a homemade alcohol drink.

You've heard of moonshine . . . raisin-jack was just as bad—or worse. The basic ingredients for it were: raisins, yeast, sugar, water, and time to ferment. Some of the deck hands would climb into the life rafts at night and put the ingredients for raisin-jack into the water kegs. After a few months of rocking in the heat of the tropical sun, they would have a powerful homemade moonshine. I'd tasted raisin-jack; a glass of it will give you the worst headache that you could possibly imagine.

A major factor in the entire process was leaving the cork in the water keg slightly ajar, so that the gases created during fermentation process could escape. Periodically the contents of the life rafts were inspected and the home brew would be found and thrown away. The officers always tried to discover who put the ingredients into the water kegs. Of course, no one knew anything.

Whoever made and stored the raisin-jack in the galley made the mistake of using a large empty glass pickle jar. He put the mixture into the jar and tightly secured the lid. Then he hid it in a small storage area located in a corner of the galley.

After over a month at sea—with the heat of the galley in tropical waters—the gases had built up so much pressure in the jar (which apparently had a slight defect in the glass), that it exploded. The echoing boom that woke up the ship sent fermented raisins and glass all over the food preparation area. Fortunately, at that time of the morning, we didn't have anyone on the duty in the area of the explosion.

Upon securing from General Quarters, all of the cooks, bakers and mess-cooks were ordered to the galley. That was when I saw the mess. Oh, did it smell from the sickening odor of fermented raisins. I didn't know what the fallout would be.

We knew that one of the new mess-cooks had been gathering the ingredients to make raisin-jack. But we never thought he would be dumb enough to use a glass pickle jar and then screw down the lid. Thank goodness I wasn't involved.

We all had to turn to in order to clean up the mess so that the duty shift could start preparing the morning meal. Chief Commissary Steward James Beavers and our commissary officer, Lieutenant M. W. Sturgis from Bell Gardens, California were livid. We didn't know anything. I had never seen our senior officers so mad. They were ordered to find out what happened and report to the captain. I didn't envy them their task. Captain Snyder had an explosive side to him. I'm glad I didn't have to go before him to try to explain what had happened. I wondered how or even if it would be written up in the ship's log.

The ex-prisoner was lucky. Knowing the ramifications of his possibly going back to prison, we suggested that one of our troop mess-cooks who had just debarked in the Philippines was responsible for making the concoction. I think the officers knew that we were covering up for the new sailor, because they transferred him off the ship at the next port.

WEDNESDAY, 7 NOVEMBER 1945
LIBERTY AT PEARL HARBOR

The last time we were at Pearl, the war in the Pacific had been building up to its critical final conclusion. The area was a flurry of activity. With the war over, reflecting back to what it was like a few months earlier, the harbor was almost empty.

Below is a copy of the information sheet issued to our crew regarding liberty hours and rules pertaining to Pearl Harbor and Honolulu. (1800 is 6 p.m.; 1830 is 6:30 p.m.; 1900 is 7 p.m. and 2200 is 10 p.m.). The officers had liberty from 9 a.m. to 10 p.m.; the non-rated enlisted men from 9 a.m. to 6 p.m.

In the spring of 1945, when we first arrived at Pearl Harbor the fleet anchorage was filled with ships and thousands of sailors. Liberty was allowed, but on a restricted basis.

Information Pearl Harbor Liberty

Officers — 0900–2200	CPO's — 0900 - 1900
Petty Officers — 0900–1830	Non Rated Men — 0900–1800

All men passing through the Navy yard gate will have to present a liberty pass and their identification card.

Remember, when on Liberty, you are a representative of your country. The naval service as a whole is judged by your appearance and conduct. Keep in the proper uniform at all times. Know when your liberty is up. Start for the bus or railroad station about an hour before you are due back. You must be back at the time your Liberty was up. The Shore Patrol often picks up men for minor offenses, such as staggering, improper uniform, jay walking, etc. Remember, the Shore Patrol has unlimited authority over personnel ashore. Carry out their orders. Don't argue with them.

The Uniform For Liberty
Officers & CPO's — Grays or Khakis with ties
Enlisted men — Undress whites with neckerchief

RECREATION FACILITIES
Officers—Kalekai at Waikiki Beach
Enlisted personnel—
        Nimitz Recreation Field and Beach at Barber Point
        The Breakers at 2707 Kalakaua Avenue
        Royal Hawaiian Hotel
        Richard's Recreation Center (located to the westward of
        Kamehameha Highway between Halawa stream and Aiea)

LIQUOR REGULATIONS
Beer and liquor will be sold to personnel in uniform by drink only. It is against the law for enlisted men to have bottled liquor in their possession at any time. Beer may be purchased before 1600 (4 p.m.) and mixed drinks between 1600 (4 p.m.) and 1800 (6 p.m.). Beer is sold in the Navy yard daily but must be consumed at the beer garden.

E.G. MORRISON
Lieutenant, USNR
Executive Officer

Usually we anchored out in the harbor, but sometimes we were fortunate enough to be tied up to a dock. In a crowded harbor, many times ships were double-or triple-stacked, which means that they were tied up next to each other.

If we anchored out in the harbor, our LCVPs were used as our liberty boats. They would carry us into the fleet landing.

After arriving into port and securing from the special sea detail, the liberty parties were announced. The ship's crew was basically divided into two sections or groups: the port section and the starboard section.

Liberty was based on your assigned section. We usually alternated port or starboard liberty. Therefore at all times at least one half of the crew was aboard ship. If an emergency occurred, we could still go to General Quarters and man the various positions to get underway or perform any duties necessary to defend or save our ship.

Prior to going ashore, we were checked to ensure that we were well groomed and wore a clean, neat liberty uniform of the day. At Pearl Harbor, because of the warm tropical weather, we always wore our whites.

As we were leaving the ship, we would present our ID and liberty cards to the officer-of-the-deck or his representative on the quarterdeck near the entrance to the gangway ladder to the liberty boat. During that process, a pharmacist's mate or a member of the quarterdeck crew would hand us a pro-kit.

We were not allowed to go ashore without a pro-kit. Venereal diseases, especially syphilis and gonorrhea, were the plagues of the fleet. To help us realize what the real world was like, we were shown graphic films of the effect and consequences of contracting venereal diseases.

For a seventeen-year-old, it certainly made an indelible impression on me. It made you stop and think: Were a few moments of scared, careless pleasure worth the potential consequences? The pro-kit program apparently was successful. Very few, if any, of the fellows that I knew came down with any diseases.

To ensure that members of the crew—especially food handlers— were clean and clear of infection, on a regular basis we would have a physical inspection for venereal disease. Each duty section would have weekly short arm inspection. As a duty group, the food handlers would report to sickbay. There the Doc (pharmacist's mate) on duty would line us up and have us drop our skivvies to check each one for gonorrhea and syphilis. Overall, it was an effective program.

After presenting our ID and liberty cards, we would walk down the gangway ladder and climb into a bobbing LCVP. When our boat was loaded, the coxswain would have his bow and stern-hooks cast off, and we would be underway for the fleet landing and liberty. What a great feeling it was after being at sea for several weeks to be able to leave the ship and go ashore!

The coxswains of the liberty boats from the ships in the harbor were like choreographed dancers as they maneuvered their crafts to and from the fleet landing docking area. They were good. Occasionally there would be an incident where one boat would bump into or ram another. But, considering the high volume of water traffic moving in, out and around the docking area, there were very few mishaps.

Once ashore we would walk over to the main gate where our ID and liberty cards were checked again by marine guards or the SP's. To supplement a small nucleus of the Shore Patrol (Navy's police officers) for the base, each ship would provide SP's.

Members of the Shore Patrol were petty officers with the ranks of coxswain (third class), second class or first class. A chief petty officer (CPO) was usually in charge of them. I never did have SP duty because the highest rank I attained was seaman first class (which was like a private first class in the Army), not quite a petty officer.

Members of the Shore Patrol wore a navy blue armband with the golden letters SP. They also wore canvas leggings or boots (as they were called from naval basic training days), and a webbed belt around their waist; they carried a small wooden baton (a night stick or billy club).

When we were on liberty we would frequently see shipmates who were pulling shore patrol duty. They usually tried to be in the area where they knew other members of the crew were drinking or trying to find women. When a shipmate got into trouble, our SP's would either straighten them out or shepherd them back to the ship. It was a good system. We took care of our own. Rarely did any of our crew get thrown into the local brig.

Once we were ashore and outside the base's main gate, the next direction usually depended on how long we'd been at sea. If we had been underway for several weeks, we would try to find a nearby store or cafe that served milk or ice cream. After a prolonged period at sea, most of us craved dairy products like ice cream or milk shakes.

At Pearl Harbor we would then take the narrow-gauge railroad train that ran from Pearl City to the railroad depot near Canal Street in the western part of Honolulu.

The railroad was constructed before the war to carry sugarcane from the western and northern side of Oahu to the port area of Honolulu. After the war started, open-air passenger cars were incorporated into the rail system. The line was then primarily used to transport Sailors and Marines from the naval base at Pearl Harbor to Honolulu.

Across the street from the railroad station was a canal. On the eastern side of the waterway was the corner of Canal and Beretania Streets. Most of the bars were along Beretania Street, and the whorehouses (before they were shut down) were located in some of the older buildings along Canal Street.

They said that most of the working girls were haloes (women from the States) and the others were primarily Filipinos. They charged three dollars for three minutes, and one dollar for each minute after. Sailors would line up out onto the sidewalk waiting for their turn to go inside.

A majority of the customers were older, from nineteen to twenty-five years old. Most of them had the pay scale of petty officers and could afford the services provided. We saw very few lower-ranking enlisted men standing in the cathouse lines.

I was seventeen-years-old. As a seaman-second-class, I only made fifty-nine dollars per month. After everything was taken out (five dollars for life insurance and eighteen dollars and seventy-five cents for a twenty-five dollar War Bond which I monthly had sent home to my mother for safe keeping) I had thirty-five dollars and twenty-five cents a month left for me spend on toothpaste, razors, candy, recreation and other personal living expenses.

The lack of money and the vivid memory of the VD films we were shown in boot camp scared most of us teenage sailors. The Navy's anti-VD program made a solid impression on us.

THE LEGAL AGE TO DRINK WAS TWENTY-ONE

The legal age to purchase liquor was supposed to be twenty-one. Beer was ten to twenty cents per glass. When we went into a bar to order a beer, if we were in uniform and had sea duty—especially combat sea

" All prices list........ are at or below
our OPA.............. "

June 16, 1945.

Mayfair, Limited.

Fruit cocktail-----------Cream of corn soup.
Soup or cocktail w ithout mea l-----------10¢

ENTREE

~~Boiled corn beef with~~ cabbage---------------50¢
Lamb currie with rice-----------------------50¢
Baked macaroni with ham---------------------45¢
Spanish omelette----------------------------50¢

ROAST

~~Roast loin of pork~~ with apple sauce--------60¢

COLD PLATE WITH POTATO SALAD

Chopped ham----------50¢   Balogne-----------40¢

SALAD (Nothing included with salad)

Potat o salad-------------------------------15¢
Shrimp salad--------------------------------40¢
Crabmeat salad------------------------------45¢

Drinks free with meal from 11 a.m to 5 p.m.
Iced tea, hot tea, orangeade, sodas in glass
and coffee.

ASK FOR FOR DESSERT

THE SMOOTHEST ICE CREAM IN TOWN

❧ M E N U ❧

SANDWICHES

On Toast Extra Charge ...... .05

Mayfair	.30	Western	.30
Cheese	.15	Clubhouse	.60
Fried Egg	.15	Manhattan	.60
Fried Ham	.15	Cold Meat	.15
Fried Egg, Island	.20	Cold Ham	.20
Hamburger	.15	Cold Pork	.20
Ham and Egg	.30	Cold Ox Tongue	.20
Chicken	.30	Sardine	.15
Tuna	.15	Hot Roast, Beef or Pork with	
Sweet Pork	.20	Mashed Potatoes	.30
New Orlean	.30	Tomato Sandwich	.15

VEGETABLES AND SAUCE

American Fried Potatoes	.15	Potato Chips	.15
French Fried Potatoes	.20	Fried Onions	.10
Hashed Brown Potatoes	.15	Sugar Corn	.20
Minced Brown Potatoes	.15	Stewed Tomatoes	.20
Lyonnaise Potatoes	.20	Sweet Peas	.20
Shoe String Potatoes	.20	Hot Asparagus, butter sauce	.45
Potato Au Gratin	.30	Spanish Sauce	.15

TOASTS AND CEREALS

Doughnuts	.10	Corn Flakes with Milk	.15
Dry Toast	.10	Carnation Wheat Flakes with	
Butter Toast	.10	Milk	.15
Milk Toast	.20	Waffle with Syrup	.20
French Toast	.30	Biscuits	.05
Muffins	.10		.15

Hot Cakes with Maple Syrup served until 10:30 A. M. ...... .15

DESSERT AND FRUIT

Fresh Papaia	.10	Stewed Prunes	.10
Banana with Cream	.15	Pie, per cut	.10
Sliced Orange	.15	Custard Pie	.15

DRINKS

Tomato Juice	.15	Grape Juice	.15
Orangeade, per glass	.05	Cold Milk, per glass	.10
Orange Juice, per glass	.15	Coffee, per cup	.05
Iced Coffee, per glass	.05	Chocolate, per cup	.10
Iced Tea, per glass	.10	Tea, per cup	.05
Lemonade, per glass	.10	Hot Milk, per cup	.15
Apple Juice	.15	Jelly	.05

Extra Butter ...... .05

Above and on opposite page: Menus from The Mayfair Cafe in Honolulu.

duty—the bartender or bouncers seldom asked about age or for any identification.

If they did ask for one, thanks to the yeomen aboard ship, most of us
that were under twenty-one had a fake ID card. That Navy ID card that
said I was born in 1923, instead of my real birth date, 1927. I was one of
the youngest looking twenty-one-year-old in the fleet!

A ROLL OF DIMES

A sailor's uniform, with a white hat and bellbottom trousers, didn't
have an article of clothing like a belt that could be used as a defensive
weapon. Marines and Soldiers wore belts as part of their uniforms. In barroom or street fights, they could whip off their belts, roll them over their
fists, and use the metal buckle as a weapon. Some of them carried knives,
but usually the belt buckles were the weapons of choice.

Even though it was against naval regulations and you could get into
trouble if you were caught, many of the sailors, myself included, would
put a roll-of-dimes in the center of our blue uniform neckerchief, fold it
lengthwise and tie the dimes in place with cotton twine. When the neckerchief was worn, the roll-of-dimes would be hidden under the back of the
uniform collar bib.

As we went through the guard checkpoints going to and from
Liberty, neither the Marines nor the SP's ever looked at my neckerchief to
see if I had a roll-of-dimes wrapped in it. The guards seemed to be primarily interested in trying to find bottles of whiskey that might possibly
be hidden in our socks or under our armpits.

In a barroom brawl or a street fight in seaports throughout the world,
the neckerchief with dimes in it made a good defensive weapon. It could
be quickly whipped off, wrapped around your hand and become a sailor's
survival tool.

Being five foot ten and weighing 145 pounds, I wasn't in the league
to be a fighter. Most of the time a group of us younger sailors went ashore
together and we pretty much watched out for each other. We were primarily five foot eight to eleven inches tall. The shipmate we usually went
with on liberty was Carlo diMaggio from San Diego, California. He was
a nice guy, good-natured, a real friend. Carlo, or as we called him,
"diMag," was about six feet tall and weighed around 200 pounds. Big and
strong, his physical presence was reassuring. Whenever there were any

fights around, we pretty much stayed on the perimeter of the conflict unless a member of the crew of the *Fergus* was involved. Then we went to help our shipmate.

HONOLULU AND WAIKIKI BEACH (DOGS AND SAILORS, KEEP OFF THE GRASS)

From the train depot most of us would walk the almost four miles to downtown Honolulu and then over to Waikiki Beach. Along the way the sidewalks and parts of the streets would be filled with a sea of white-hatted sailors in their white uniforms. The businesses along the way were a conglomeration of stands like at a seedy carnival. They had almost every type of enticement that could be thought of to separate a sailor from his money.

The area was sprinkled with bars, tattoo parlors, penny arcades and photo shops. In the photo shops, you could have your photograph taken with your shipmates for fifty cents, or, for an extra twenty-five cents, a photo of you hugging a pretty little Hawaiian gal. They were cuties. Most of the times, we had pictures taken with our shipmates so that we could send the souvenir snap shots home to our parents or friends.

On our way to downtown Honolulu, we were encouraged to remain on the main thoroughfares. They cautioned us to stay off the side streets. The locals were not happy to have sailors wandering around their residential neighborhoods.

The younger Hawaiian males were very protective of their teenage sisters. Sailors on liberty were like a pack of dogs on the loose. If a white-hat strayed into the wrong neighborhood, it was not uncommon to have several of the young local males beat him up. We were an inconvenience of necessity. The attitude in the residential neighborhoods was that naval enlisted personnel should stay away; we were not welcome. In fact some of the smaller parks had signs saying "Dogs and Sailors, Keep off the Grass."

The Royal Hawaiian Hotel was our usual destination. It affectionately was called the Pink Palace because of its exterior color. The hotel was beautiful, especially the entrance grounds approaching the lobby. Naval enlisted personnel were allowed to use the beach in front of the hotel and its public facilities.

The rooms were reserved for submarine enlisted men that had just returned from war patrols and for aircraft carrier flight crews. I never heard any remarks like, "Why are they the only ones that get to stay at the Royal Hawaiian?" We knew that those sailors had paid their dues and more than earned the special privileges that they received.

The other hotel on Waikiki Beach was the Moana. It was an older, classic looking wooden building closer to Diamond Head, the extinct volcano landmark for the island of Oahu. They said the Moana was reserved for officers. We enlisted men were told to stay away from the area around the hotel.

During the war, Waikiki Beach had barbed wire strung along potential invasion landing areas. In front of the Royal Hawaiian Hotel, a section of the barbed wire was placed into the surf. That was the area where we could go into the water. Its temperature was wonderful—a lot warmer than we had back home in Northern California.

We had to be back aboard ship by 1800 (6 p.m.). Around 1500 to 1600 (3 to 4 p.m.), depending upon how far we were away from the train depot, we would start walking in that direction.

Many times, if we were hungry and still had some money, we would stop by a great Chinese restaurant named Woo Fats. It was located upstairs in a colorfully painted building with Chinese decor. The food was good and the prices were affordable, especially with our dwindled funds.

Around 1600, (4 p.m.), from all over Honolulu, white-hatted sailors began converging on the train depot for the ride back to Pearl Harbor. On the corner of Canal and Beretania Streets was a bar called Sad Sam's. If you wanted a drink, this watering hole was usually the first pit stop for liberty parties and one of the last if you wanted to have "one for the road " before boarding the train.

Sad Sam's was quite a place. In the morning it wasn't too bad, but by the late afternoon, it could get wild. The frustration and nastiness of some of the mean drunks would emerge. Fights were a fairly common occurrence.

The SP's would stand around waiting for trouble. They did a good job of keeping everything under control and shepherding the sailors back to the safety of their ships.

One afternoon after liberty in Honolulu, some of my shipmates and I we started to go into the Beretania Street side entrance to Sad Sam's. Suddenly a sailor lunged out of the door with his hands clasped over his

Honolulu, 1945 and 1946. Above, Jim Reding on left, and Melvin Norman. Below, Diamond Head.

stomach. Blood was oozing from between his fingers. There had been an argument. The guy he had been arguing with stuck a knife into him and cut his stomach wide open.

Fortunately there were some pharmacist's mates in the area. They gave him first aid and the SP's arranged transportation for the injured sailor to receive further medical treatment. I don't know what ever happened to the fellow. A knifing like that could be so fast. From the look on his face, I don't think the poor devil knew what happened to him. I hope he survived.

When we finally arrived back at the main gate checkpoint at the fleet landing, the marine guards would check our ID and liberty cards, and anything we were carrying. Some of the sailors were continually trying to put something over on them by trying to bring back half pints or pints of whatever kind of booze they could find. A sailor's uniform was usually formfitting; it was difficult to hide anything in your pockets or blouse. But we did have bell-bottom trousers.

The Navy's enlisted man's uniform was functional. Everything seemed to be designed around the concept of survival at sea. The white-hat could be used to capture air and keep you afloat. Also, the bell-bottoms on the trousers made them more easily removed in the water so that knots could be tied in the legs. Then the knotted trousers could be thrown over your shoulder to capture a sufficient quantity of air to form a kind of water-wing flotation device.

I never did find out the reasoning behind the front flap of our dress blue trousers. They said that the thirteen buttons represented the original thirteen colonies. After a while, we got pretty good at buttoning and unbuttoning them with one hand.

The flare on the bellbottom trousers was ideal to help hide a small bottle of whiskey in a sailor's socks on the inside of the pants leg. Sometimes the sailors would be able to make it past the Marine or SP guards at the gate, but most of the time, the wary Marines or SP's could instinctively spot a bottle carrier.

As the sailor approached the gate, the guard would have him stand with his legs spread about a foot apart. The guard, usually a Marine, would quickly move his billy-club back and forth in the ankle area of the trousers. If their instincts were good—and they frequently were—the clink of the billy-club striking the glass bottles would be heard.

The guard would have the sailor remove the bottle or bottles from his socks and hand them over. If the gate guard was a nice guy, he would just take the bottles over to a trash can, break them in front of the sailor and let him go to his ship. If he wasn't a nice guy, the sailor would usually end up in the brig with an Executive Officer's Mast. That could mean a six-month delay in being eligible to take the test for promotion, and extra duty for a few weeks.

Liberty always seemed to be an adventure. Most of the time, we felt relieved to get back to the comfort and security of our ship. She was our home.

THE USO

The USO (United Services Organization) was a wonderful civilian service for the Armed Forces. It was established to help military personnel have a semblance of a home away from home. They were located in almost every community within close proximity of a military base.

In December 1944, when we were in San Pedro, California I had the privilege of visiting the USO in Hollywood. It was popularly known as the Hollywood Canteen. I saw a lot of very nice people who really worked hard to make our liberties more enjoyable. The atmosphere and entertainment was great. The food was excellent and the people were very friendly. They said that the Hollywood Canteen was the place to see the stars, but I never saw any.

On Guam, in the Mariana Islands, with its tropical heat and humidity, we were fortunate to see a USO show in an outdoor theater. The performers were an old-time vaudeville song-and-dance man plus some young women who were great singers and dancers. They put on a wonderful performance.

We never did see any stars. I guess the stars were out there, but the only ones we saw were up in the sky. In the military you live in two worlds. One is for the big ships, officers and the selected ones. Then there is the world for the rest of us.

BECOMING A WATCH-CAPTAIN

In February 1946, our assignment was changed. We were no longer on the Magic Carpet returning personnel to the States. Rumors were that we were slated for decommissioning. The ship's company was reduced from 287 enlisted men to a crew of less than 200.

Due to the point system, when our cooks (second and third class petty officers) transferred off the ship for their return to civilian life, we received replacement cooks aboard.

At that time, I was six months past my eighteenth birthday and still a seaman first class. I was a "Plank Owner" who had been aboard ship for over a year. The chief knew me and my capabilities, but he didn't know the two replacements. Both of the replacements were petty officers, one a second class and the other a third class. They were also a couple of years older than me.

Soon after the new crewmen reported aboard ship, Chief Commissary Steward Jim Beavers called me aside and asked me if I wanted to be a watch-captain. In that position, it would be my responsibility to feed approximately 200 men three meals a day. I told him "Yes!" If he thought I could do the job, I was willing to try my best. He had confidence in me, which in turn gave me confidence in myself.

Chief Beavers, with the concurrence of Mr. Sturgis, our division officer, named me as a watch-captain and assigned one of the new senior-ranking cooks to work for me. Even though he was two ranks above me, he didn't object. For over four months prior to leaving the ship, I was the starboard watch-captain in the galley. In the military you grow up fast.

I had been aboard the *Fergus* since it was commissioned over a year and a half before. I was bored and wanted a change of duty. In April 1946, I applied for transfer to another ship and requested China duty. My request was denied.

Even though I was just an eighteen-year-old seaman first class cook's striker, Mr. Sturgis stated that I was "essential" because I was a watch-captain in the galley . . . "cannot be spared." It was hard to believe—a cook's striker being declared essential.

NOB-SP—4-10-45—5M

U. S. S. Fergus A.P.A. 82

ALL REQUESTS MUST BE SUBMITTED TO EXECUTIVE OFFICERS' OFFICE
PRIOR TO 1000

SPECIAL REQUEST
Date March 11, 1946 , 194

REDING, JAMES JOHN   S1/c
(Name—Surname First)   (Rate)   (Billet No.)

It is requested that I be granted:

_____Regular leave-   _____Permission to stop allotment-

_____Emergency leave-   _____Special request-

_____Special liberty-   X Transfer-

_____Exchange of liberty-

From: _____ To: _____
(Time and date)   (Time and date)

Reason: Desire China Duty for the rest of my time
in the Navy which is until June 15, 1946. Believe
I need a change of duty. I have been aboard since
commissioning.

My address on leave will be _____

I am (not) in the liberty section.

I have had _____ days leave this calendar year (not counting re-
enlistment leave).

My standby who is in the liberty section is:

_____   _____
(Signature of Standby)   (Billet No.)

Not Recommended: (If approval is not recommended state reason.)
Watch captain in galley cannot be spared
M W Sturgo
(Division Officer)

_____Recommended: (If approval is not recommended state reason.)

_____
(Head of Department)

Statements verified: _____
(Yeoman)

_____ Approved. JF Wheeler
(Executive Officer)

NSD-SP-O.D. 27

CHAPTER XII

OPERATIONS DOWNFALL AND CROSSROADS

After the war was over, we learned that in the spring of 1943, under the Command of General George Marshall, the Joint Chiefs of Staff had drawn up a master plan for the defeat of the Japanese. This plan was named Operation Downfall. It was divided into two segments that called for the invasion of Kyushu, Japan's southernmost large island, in the fall of 1945, and the invasion of Japan's main island of Honshu in the spring of 1946.

The overall plan was initiated in 1943. The primary features were to recapture the Philippines, which were accomplished in the latter part of 1944, and the first part of 1945, and the establishment of air bases within flight proximity of the main islands of Japan. This was done with the invasion and capture of Guam, Saipan, Tinian, (September–October 1944) Iwo Jima (February–March 1945) and Okinawa (April–June 1945).

The Japanese homeland is comprised of over 3,000 islands. Within the group are four large or major islands. The largest and most heavily populated is Honshu, which has the capital, Tokyo. The invasion of Honshu was scheduled for the spring of 1946.

Prior to Honshu, the islands south of it had to be seized or neutralized. On November 1, 1945, under the code name Operation Olympic, the island of Kyushu was to be invaded. The *Fergus* was scheduled to be part of that invasion fleet.

According to the plan, a task force of 2,000 ships was scheduled to transport 800,000 men to the beaches of Kyushu on D-Day. That invasion armada would have been more than twice the size of the June 1944

Normandy landings on the coast of France.

The initial attack was scheduled to have three prongs or invasion areas. The 5th Marine Amphibious Corps would land on Kyushu's southeast coast. The United States Army's 11th Corps would land on Paliaki Bay and the Army's 1st Corps would invade the southwest coast.

Providing air cover to protect such a huge amphibious task force would be 2,500 carrier-based aircraft, plus thousands of land-based aircraft from airfields on Guam, Saipan, Tinian, Iwo Jima, the Philippines, China, Ie Shima and Okinawa.

The planned staging areas (assembly points) for the troops and ships for the all-out offensive thrust would have been: Tacloban on Leyte and Manila on Luzon in the Philippines; Guam, Saipan and Tinian in the Marianas; Ulithi in the Caroline Islands; Iwo Jima in the Bonin Islands; plus Pearl Harbor and Maui in the Hawaiian Islands. Also some ships and men would have come from Australia.

With home bases thousands of miles from the battlefields, supplying and sustaining such a gigantic military force would have been an enormously complex logistical challenge. This massive invasion task force would be the largest fleet in the history of naval warfare. Without the atomic bomb, the beaches and waters off the coast of Kyushu would have run red with the blood of young Americans and Japanese.

For the three-pronged invasion of the island of Kyushu, the estimated casualties would have been around one million Allied and Japanese personnel, killed or wounded. The planners projected that the opposition would be so ferocious that within a few weeks of fighting, the entire 5th Marine Amphibious Corps would be so decimated that—without heavy reinforcements—they would virtually cease to exist as an effective fighting unit.

The Japanese defensive objective was to sink or damage our troopships before we could land our personnel on the beaches. A massive Kamikaze banzai attack by aircraft, small boats and submarines would have the task of inflicting maximum damage on our fleet as it approached the Japanese homeland.

As a troopship, we would have been one of the enemy's prime targets. I wonder if the *Fergus* and any of us on her would have survived the carnage, or if today we would be just names on a memorial wall.

OPERATION CROSSROADS
APRIL 1946. SAN PEDRO, CALIFORNIA

The *Fergus* became part of the fleet that was being prepared for the first over-and-under- water nuclear explosions. These atomic experiments were designated as Operation Crossroads. The tests were to be held in the Central Pacific Ocean at Bikini Atoll, in the Marshall Islands.

We had been to Eniwetok and Kwajalein in the Marshall Islands, but not to Bikini. If it was anything like "Wetok" or "Kwaj", there wasn't much there. It would be just a lagoon surrounded by small picturesque coral atolls covered with coconut trees.

In preparation for the tests preliminary modifications were made to our ship at the naval shipyard in San Pedro, California. At San Pedro, we tied up on the outboard side of the battleship USS *Nevada* (BB 36). It was a classic old-time warrior.

The *Nevada* was being painted chromite red, which is an orange-red color. It was certainly strange to see a red battleship. The old warrior was destined to go down in the history books as the target ship for the first over-water atomic bomb explosion.

Whenever we went ashore, we walked cross the battleship's beautiful teakwood decks. The planks on those decks were cleaned by using blocks of soft sandstone to hand scrub or "holystone" the wood. Standing on the *Nevada*, I could easily imagine groups of lower-level enlisted men on their knees holystoning the beautiful teakwood. I was glad to be a ship's cook.

In San Pedro, the guns on our ship along with all of its wartime gear, basic equipment and non-essential items were removed. We were becoming a skeleton of ourselves.

Assorted sizes of steel cages were constructed and welded onto the decks throughout the exterior portions of the ship. They told us that the cages were for live animals such as goats, pigs and dogs that would be part of the test.

The USS *Burelson* (APA 67), a sister ship of the *Fergus*, was being modified and converted to transport the animals which would be used in the experiment. We were told that scientists wanted to find out what effect an atomic explosion had on living creatures at different distances from the center point of the blast.

MAY AND JUNE 1946

In May the *Fergus* sailed from San Pedro, California to Pearl Harbor for the ship's final preparations before going to Bikini. At Pearl Harbor, a major segment of the fleet destined to participate in the Operation Crossroads atomic bomb tests was being assembled. We tied up near the submarine base where additional modifications were made to our ship before it was scheduled to sail to the Marshall Islands.

At Pearl Harbor, I had the opportunity to go aboard the German cruiser *Prinz Eugen* (IX 30), which was part of

USS Nevada *(BB36) target ship for A-bomb tests.*

the fleet going to Bikini. A fellow I knew from high school was a member of the US Navy crew that sailed the ship from the Atlantic Ocean to Pearl Harbor. He asked me if I wanted to come aboard and look around. It was quite an opportunity and I said yes.

As I toured the *Prinz Eugen*, it was obvious that the Germans had constructed a warship that was technologically superior to our vessels. It was like comparing a custom-built automobile versus one that was mass-produced on an assembly line. The living conditions for the German enlisted men seemed to be more Spartan than the accommodations we had aboard the *Fergus*.

We heard that there were going to be two nuclear devices (atomic bombs) exploded. One was going to be an airdrop from one of our bombers and the other was going to be an under water detonation.

We thought the airdrop would create a huge fireball with intense heat and a typhoon type wind like at Hiroshima. For the underwater explosion, we speculated that it would cause a tsunami (giant tidal wave). No one mentioned anything about radiation or radioactive fallout.

In July 1946, at Bikini Atoll in the Marshall Islands, most of the ships that were assembled at Pearl Harbor became part of history. They were among the vessels that were subjected to the first over and under water atomic explosions. The devastating destructiveness of those Operation Crossroads nuclear weapons is frequently seen in photographs and documentaries.

Pearl Harbor, May 1946. Twin stackers that were part of the atomic bomb fleet.

CHAPTER XIII

LEAVING THE *FERGUS*
AND GOING HOME

LEAVING THE *FERGUS*

With so much sea duty, by June 1, 1946, I had accumulated sufficient points to be eligible for a discharge from active duty. Being a ship's cook, I was considered essential personnel. Mr. Sturgis, our division officer, offered me a promotion to third-class-petty-officer if I would extend my enlistment for three months. He said I would be a crew-member on one of the ships going to Bikini.

I was eighteen years old. In the almost twenty months that I had been aboard the *Fergus*, I had only one three days leave (when I had my appendix removed). With over one year and a half of almost continually being at sea, I was tired. I told him I would rather go home.

Five days later I was transferred off the *Fergus* to the enlisted barracks at the Submarine Base at Pearl Harbor. There, I waited for transportation back to the nearest Port of Entry in the United States. Hawaii was then still a territory.

Leaving the *Fergus* was an experience filled with deep mixed emotions. I was happy to be able to go home, yet I felt like I was leaving a friend. I had been aboard her since she was commissioned. I was a "plank owner." She was my ship.

It was sad to see such a grand lady tied up to the dock, stripped of her guns and most of her equipment. With torn reluctance, I walked down the gangway, turned and took a long look at her, and walked away. I couldn't look back; there were too many memories. That was the last time that I saw her. She was a good ship.

USS Fergus *(APA 82).*

Decades later I learned that she was not needed as one of the vessels for the atomic bomb tests. A few days after I left the *Fergus*, she was decommissioned where she was berthed at the sub base docking area. Several months later, she was unglamorously towed to California and anchored in a portion of San Francisco Bay as part of the mothball fleet of surplus ships. At that time I was living in San Jose, less than seventy-five miles away. I did not know that she was anchored there or I would have tried to visit her. She was an important part of my life. In 1948 she was sold for scrap.

GOING HOME

After two days at the Submarine base, I was assigned to an outgoing draft. On June 5, 1946, we went aboard the USS *Arthur Middleton* (APA 25). Aboard the ship, were over 1,000 passengers. Some of them were women and children dependents. The rest of us were military personnel being returned to the States for reassignment or discharge from the service.

On the *Middleton*, I learned what it was like being a passenger on a troopship, with its long chow lines and salt-water showers.

It took us seven days to sail from the Hawaiian Islands to the coast of California. A few hours before dawn on June 12, 1946, we reached a position just south of the Farallon Islands, where we waited.

With the first sign of daylight, the captain gave the orders for the ship to proceed ahead at standard speed. We began moving toward the California coastline and the Golden Gate entrance to San Francisco Bay.

Wednesday morning, June 12, 1946, was one of those special days in a person's life. After a restless night of trying to sleep, I was out of my bunk at 0500 (5 a.m.). I shaved the peach fuzz off my face, and hopefully took my last salt-water shower.

In the semi-darkness of the troop compartment, I put on my dress blues uniform, packed my sea bag, rolled up the ship's mattress and placed it on the end of the laced canvas bunk. By 0545 (5:45 a.m.), shaved, showered and wearing shiny shoes, I was ready to go ashore.

At 0600 (6 a.m.) the familiar click of the on-button of the ship's PA system was easily heard. Then came the sound of the boatswain's pipe announcing reveille. It was time for all ship's personnel and passengers to wake up, get up, and start the day.

No breakfast for me that morning. Rather than going to the mess hall for chow, I went topside. After months of living in the oppressive heat of the tropics, standing on the main deck in the crisp morning fog was refreshing.

There must had been 200 other white-hat sailors standing with me on the starboard side of the forecastle (the front portion of the ship). We were all straining our eyes to catch that first glimpse of sunrise, landfall and home.

Faintly, through the dim light of dawn, there it was, the outline of the rocky outcropping of the California coastline. Then in the distance, slowly growing larger through the morning mist was the majestic Golden Gate Bridge. The silhouette was beautifully outlined in the glowing crimson rays of the rising sun.

Just outside the entrance to the bay, a small pilot boat came bobbing toward us. As the boat was pulling alongside, our crew hung a Jacob's ladder over the side of the ship. With the agility of an acrobat the pilot grasped a rung of the swaying ladder and climbed aboard.

With the pilot in command of the helm, our speed was increased and we proceeded toward the entrance channel, under the bridge and into the bay.

Off the starboard bow we saw the remnants of the Civil War army base called Fort Point. Next were the airstrip and hangars for Crissy Field Army Air Corps Base. Beyond the airstrip were the mustard colored buildings of Fort Mason Army Base with its docks and warehouses. Behind Crissy Field and Fort Mason stood the beautiful silhouetted skyline of the City of San Francisco. It was hard to believe that we were back home.

The bay was very busy. It certainly lived up to its reputation of being one of the major seaports in the world. An interesting sight to see were the small tugboats as they gently nudged large ships into and out of the docking area along the waterfront.

And then, there they were—the cumbersome white ferryboats shuttling to and from the docking area at the Ferry Building located at the foot of Market Street. The boats moved passengers and vehicles from San Francisco to Oakland and other landing destinations around the bay.

Proudly perched on one of the rocky knolls along the Embarcadero was the Coit Tower. It was protectively watching over the city and its waterfront. Shaped like the nozzle of an old-fashioned fireman's hose, the Tower was and still is one of the city's prominent landmarks. Reportedly it was designed and constructed to honor the firemen that saved San Francisco from the devastating fire, which followed the Great Earthquake of 1906.

Behind Coit Tower, on the crest of Nob Hill, were the Mark Hopkins and the Fairmont Hotels. The Mark Hopkins Hotel had a restaurant and a bar on the top (twenty-first) floor called the Sky Room. The Sky Room was said to be one of San Francisco's in-places. It was suppose to have the finest views of the city, the bay and the Golden Gate Bridge.

During the war, the Top of the Mark was a popular meeting place and hangout for naval officers—especially for aviators from carriers anchored in the Bay and at the naval air station on Alameda Island. The Mark was definitely "Officers' Country."

Behind the bar, individual aviation squadrons would have a special bottle with the squadron's name and design logo proudly displayed on the label. At the Mark, there was a tradition that any naval aviator could go to the bar and order a drink from his squadron's bottle for no charge. The only catch was, if your drink was the last one poured from the bottle, you had to purchase a new full bottle for your squadron from the bar, at bar prices, That could turn out to be a very expensive "free" drink.

But they were either going to, or had just returned from the war zone. With the realities of the dangers involved in taking off and landing on carriers at sea under normal operational—much less combat—conditions, coupled with the high casualty rates being suffered by Navy aviators, what value did money really have?

The northwest corner of the Top of the Mark offered a magnificent view of the Golden Gate Bridge and the ships as they left the protective haven of San Francisco Bay to go to war. So many tears were shed by loved ones watching the ships carrying their men sail out beneath the Golden Gate Bridge, and not knowing if they would ever return, that the northwestern corner of the Mark was referred to as "Weepers Corner."

Months after the conclusion of hostilities, for those that could afford the luxury, a common phrase in the fleet was "Meet you at the Top of the Mark."

ALCATRAZ AND TREASURE ISLAND— HOME AT LAST

As we proceeded into the bay, off our port bow was the Federal Prison on Alcatraz Island, more commonly known as "The Rock." They announced over the ship's PA system that—just a little over a month before—on May 2, 1946, prisoners had captured some guards and tried to escape from the prison.

A marine detachment from Treasure Island landed on "The Rock" and, after a gun battle, subdued the prisoners. You could still see the pock-marked scars from the firefight.

From Alcatraz, we approached the San Francisco Bay Bridge and our destination, Treasure Island (TI). It seemed like yesterday, even though it was six years earlier when I was twelve years old, that my mother and I had attended the 1939 World's Fair right there on Treasure Island.

The war had certainly changed the island. Some of the pavilion buildings were still standing, but most of the land was being used for barracks, warehouses, docking areas, fire fighting school and the other facilities usually found on an active United States naval base.

Two tugboats came out to meet us. They pulled alongside and gently began nudging our ship into the assigned berthing area. There was a feeling of electricity in the air. Eagerly we waited for the lines to be secured and the gangway to be put into place. Some of the passengers aboard ship had not been in the States for years. It almost seemed like a dream; it was hard to believe that we were really in California, soon to be processed for discharge and returned to civilian life.

After the ship's lines were doubled up securing us to the docking area, the gangway was lowered into position. Over the ship's PA came the Attention All Hands call from the boatswain's pipe followed by orders for,

"All passengers to report with bag and hammock to your muster stations for disembarkation."

I went below to my bunk in the troop passenger quarters to get my sea bag. In my sea bag were all my worldly possessions, which consisted of a mattress cover, sheets, a blanket, work shoes, socks, skivvies, blue dungarees, a white uniform, a pea coat, my sheathed knife, a shaving kit and a few personal items.

As a sailor in the United States Navy, I wore the white stripe of a seaman on the right-shoulder of my dress blue uniform. On my cuffs were the three white stripes indicating that I was a seaman first class. On the left side of my chest, above my uniform pocket, was a row of three campaign ribbons for service in the American Theater of Operations, the Asiatic-Pacific, and the Philippine Campaigns.

For the past twenty months I had been aboard my ship. A major portion of that time was in the far western Pacific. We had crossed the Pacific Ocean twice during the war and three times after the war was over.

Many times, there were moments when I didn't think that I would live to be a civilian again. It was hard to believe that I was still only eighteen years old and was going to be able to go home.

With all of that sea duty, I was still only a seaman first class, just two ranks above a recruit, in other words, not exactly career material. I wasn't alone; there were a lot of my shipmates on the same worker level. We had just wanted to do our duty and go back home to civilian life.

Our section aboard the troop ship was called for departure. We gathered in formation on deck with all of our gear, ready to leave the ship. When it was our turn, we proceeded down the gangway with our sea bags on our shoulders.

Then we reached the bottom of the steps . . . what a wonderful feeling it was to set foot on the dock and realize that we were really back in the States and home!

A couple of the sailors actually dropped down on their knees, placed their hands on the warm asphalt-covered wooden planking of the dock, and gave it a big kiss. We all had smiles on our faces, and there were even twinkles in the tired young eyes that had seen so much.

On the docks, we were formed up into squads and marched over to the base Receiving Ship where we were assigned sleeping accommodations in our temporary quarters.

After putting my sea bag on my bunk, the Non-Commissioned-Officer-In-Charge (NCOIC) said we could have a half hour to get cleaned up or make to telephone calls.

Most of us headed for the pay telephones. I was one of the first ones in line, ready to make that collect call home. When it was my turn, I picked up the receiver and the operator came on the line. I asked her to place a collect call to my folks in San Jose. Their telephone number was Columbia 156 M. I was hoping someone would be home.

We had a party line where we shared the telephone service with another family living in our apartment building. Ours was a two-party line, which meant that it was less likely to be busy than those with four or six party service. After two rings, which was the signal that the call was for my family, I could hear my mother say hello, and yes, she would accept my collect call.

It was so nice to hear her voice. I told Mom I was on Treasure Island, in San Francisco Bay. She had thought that I was still at Pearl Harbor on the Island of Oahu in the Hawaiian Islands.

I told her that I had enough points to be eligible for discharge from active duty. I was home to be processed for separation from the service. She was thrilled.

She told me that everyone in the family—my thirteen-year-old brother Pat, my nine-year-old sister Margie, my Dad, and my dog, Boots—was fine. She also said that I was going to graduate from high school the next night. I didn't understand what she meant.

Mom said that she had written to me last month to let me know that I was going to be awarded my high school diploma. What a surprise! I never received her letter. It must still be somewhere out there in the Pacific.

We had been on the move so much, and our mail delivery was so erratic, that some of the letters that I had received just before leaving the ship in Pearl Harbor were five and six months old. Mom told me that—because of the General Educational Development (GED) test I'd taken—they were going to give me my diploma.

Mom said that several weeks ago she had received notification from Mr. Curtis Davis, the principal of San Jose High School, informing her that I had taken the test and my score was strong enough for the board of trustees to award me my high school diploma. Mr. Davis also said that the diploma was going to be presented at the graduation ceremony for the class of June 1946. If I was unavailable, she was invited to attend the ceremony and accept the diploma for me.

My entire family was planning on attending the graduation. It was going to be held in the San Jose Civic Auditorium on San Carlos Street. I told Mom that I was waiting for shipment to a separation center to be processed to civilian status. I would see if I could get a special liberty.

There were quite a few other men standing in line waiting to make their telephone calls home, so I had to hurry and hang up. Before saying goodbye, I told Mom I would see if I could get a special liberty and I would get back to her.

It seemed like Christmas in June—take a test for several hours and receive credit for a year and a half of sitting in classrooms. That was great. I guess they didn't know what to do with us once we received our discharges and went back to civilian life. I was sure they didn't want us to go back to the local high schools and sit in classrooms with all of those young kids. I was really surprised and felt very fortunate that they were going to award me a high school diploma.

After our break time was up, we formed into squads and marched over to an administration building for processing. When it was my turn to be interviewed and assigned to a separation center, I requested permission from the processing yeoman to speak to the officer in charge for the purpose of obtaining a Special Liberty. The yeoman wanted to know why. I told him. He said great, and sent me over to another building.

After repeating my request to the NCOIC, I was then allowed to see the officer responsible for incoming transit personnel. The NCOIC gave him an update on my status that I had just arrived back in the States aboard the *Arthur Middleton* for discharge from the Navy. I then told the officer about the telephone call to my mother in San Jose, the background regarding the GED Test, and the surprise of being able to receive my high school diploma the next night at the graduation ceremony.

The lieutenant smiled and said congratulations. He then told me that the usual procedure for incoming overseas personnel slated for discharge was to have each man transferred to a separation center nearest his hometown. This had to be done as soon as the man was processed through the base receiving ship. My separation center would be Camp Shoemaker, near Pleasanton, which was not far from San Jose.

Since it was my high school graduation, and my home was only fifty miles away, the lieutenant arranged for me to have a special liberty pass that would allow me to be processed for transfer to Camp Shoemaker next Monday instead of tomorrow. That was wonderful.

CHAPTER XIV

GRADUATION FROM HIGH SCHOOL

The next morning, Thursday, June 13, 1946, wearing my dress blues uniform with campaign ribbons on my chest, and carrying on my shoulder my sea bag containing my worldly possessions, I boarded a Navy bus for the ride across the Bay Bridge from TI to San Francisco. With excited anticipation and apprehension, I was on my way to San Jose and home. They let me off at the Greyhound bus depot at Third and Howard Streets. At the bus depot, I made another collect call to my folks and told them I was on my way home.

When the bus arrived in San Jose, my folks—along with my brother and sister—were waiting for me. It was wonderful to see their smiling faces. We got into the family car, and they drove me home. As we turned into the alley next to our apartment at 14 East Reed Street, it was touching to see two small one-star flags hanging in the front window of our home. The flag with a gold star was for my mother's brother, Uncle Charlie, who was killed in 1942 in the South Atlantic. The flag with a blue star was for me.

As my Dad opened the door, there was my dog Boots waiting for me. It had been a long time. She looked at me like I was a stranger, and then cautiously she began walking toward me, sniffing with her wet nose. Then her tail began to wag and you could see the happiness in her body when she remembered who I was. What a wonderful greeting she gave me. I felt like a farmer's salt block after she got through welcoming me home.

I called the girl I had been dating before I went into the Navy. On my boot camp leave, we had agreed that she should go out on dates because I didn't know whether or not I would be coming back. We wrote to each other for several months, the letters then stopped. She answered the

Margie and Jim Reding on Jim's high school graduation day.

phone. I told her that I was back home. She said wonderful. I asked her if she was going to the graduation, the response was no. She had transferred to a high school on the other side of town, was going steady, and they were planning on getting married.

It was a disappointment. I really liked her, but couldn't blame her for going on with her life. I might as well try to get used to changes, because there would be a lot of them.

Mom fixed us a bite to eat, and then we went to the San Jose Municipal Auditorium on West San Carlos at Market Street for the graduation ceremony.

Approaching the entrance area, I felt awkward. All of the future graduates wearing their black caps and gowns were milling around, talking and laughing. I walked toward them wearing my white hat and navy blue sailor suit. Some of them looked at me, wondering who I was. I really felt out of place. They all looked so young and happy.

Sam Della Maggiore, one of my former teachers, came up and said hello. It was nice to see Big Sam. He made me feel comfortable and he told me what to do. Some of the students knew me, but I didn't know them. They were friendly and curious. The teachers lined us up alphabetically, and we began the processional march to take our places on the stage.

After we were seated—looking out at the faces of the parents, relatives and friends of the graduates—I could see my folks, my brother and my sister. They looked so happy. It was nice to be home and to be with them again.

It was a large class. I didn't know very many of the students. Most of the graduates had been half a year to a year behind me when I was going to school. You seemed to know the people in your class and the classes ahead of you, but seldom knew the students in the grades behind you.

I felt like a stranger. There I was with these kids about my age, but they looked so young, so protected and so vulnerable. For the past two years, they had been doing all of the things that high school kids did . . . going to class, high school proms, the beach at Santa Cruz, playing football and just having a good time.

During that same period of time, I had been at sea. I felt closer to my former shipmates than I did to my former classmates. Actually, I'd spent more time on my ship than I did going San Jose High School. If anyone asked me what high school I attended, I almost feel like saying the USS *Fergus*.

The commencement program contained the names of the 368 graduates, more females than males. There were sixty-five military graduates like me. During peacetime most classes had close to a fifty-fifty balance, males and females. Due to the draft and the war the males who under normal conditions would have been in school were in the military.

It was a young person's war. Of the sixty-five that were listed as military graduates, there were only four of us there in uniform to receive our diplomas. For the sixty-one who could not be there, parents or relatives received their diplomas for them. Sitting near me was a Marine who just graduated from boot camp and a sailor who had just completed a service school. The third was a Soldier stationed at an army base near San Jose. None of them had been out of the States.

While aboard the Middleton on our way from Pearl Harbor back to the States, we were given information regarding our return to civilian life and our rights as former servicemen. One of the major benefits emphasized was called the GI Bill of Rights. Aboard the *Fergus*, Mr. Tipton and Mr. Cummins told us about this benefit. As a veteran enrolled in an approved college—through the GI Bill—the government would pay for part or even all of our tuition and would also give us monthly subsistence money.

OFFICE OF PRINCIPAL

San Jose High School
Sixth and San Fernando Streets

SAN JOSE, 14, CALIFORNIA
June 7, 1946

Mr. and Mrs. John H. Reding
14 East Reed Street
San Jose, 12, California

Dear Mr. and Mrs. Reding:

Congratulations to you on the graduation of your son, James.
I know that his accomplishments have made you very happy, and I wish
for him continued success.

Since it may not be possible for him to attend the Graduation
Exercises, I should like to extend an invitation to you to be present and
receive his diploma.

Please present the enclosed tickets at the door, indicate that
you are a parent of one of the graduates in service, and the usherette
will direct you to a seat which will be reserved for you. When your
son's name is called, will one of you please step to the platform and
accept it.

I would appreciate a call to Columbia 754, indicating whether
or not you will be able to attend. I am interested in knowing your
son's rank and service in which he is serving, or has served, his country.
I wish to announce it from the stage.

If it is possible for James to be present, we would very
much appreciate having him participate in the graduation exercises
in his uniform. Please inform me if he will be able to do so.

I hope it will be possible for you or James to be with us on
Thursday, June 13.

Sincerely yours,

Curtis Davis
Principal

ao

The amount that we would receive for subsistence was based on whether we were married, had children, or were single. I was single; therefore I was entitled to receive seventy-five dollars per month for living expenses. Seventy-five dollars a month was nine dollars more than the sixty-six dollars I'd received as a seaman-first-class—with sea pay. That was great. With my high school GED diploma, I would then be eligible to attend college.

The girl sitting next to me on the stage asked me where I was stationed. I told her that I'd just arrived back in the States for discharge from the Navy. She wanted to know what I was going to do when I got out. I told her that I was receiving my high school diploma through the GED test that I took aboard ship, and I would like to go to college, but didn't know if one would accept me. She suggested San Jose State, our local state college. She said her brother—like me—had left school early and received a GED. He'd applied and was accepted. It was a good idea.

CHAPTER XV

RETURNING TO CIVILIAN LIFE

Ihad been on active duty for twenty-two months. Almost twenty of those months were aboard ship. At one-and-one-half-points per month, I had accumulated more points than many of the active duty personnel who were stationed in one of the forty-eight states. Duty within the continental limits was considered to be far less dangerous than being stationed aboard a ship or being overseas in combat zones.

Even though some of the men might have been several years older and were in the service for up to three years, because of my shipboard and over-seas duty, I was eligible for discharge before them. To some of the older soldiers and sailors, the point system didn't seem to be fair, but it was.

During our processing at the separation center, we were told to look to the future. If we dwelled on the past, we would be walking around feeling sorry for ourselves, which was not good. We should focus on looking forward to what could be, rather than what might have been.

THE RUPTURED DUCK

After receiving my high school diploma and having a grateful weekend at home, I returned to Treasure Island. From TI, a Navy bus took a detachment of us to Camp Shoemaker—near Pleasanton, California—for processing to civilian life. As a brand new civilian with an Honorable Discharge from the United States Navy, I was entitled to wear an insignia popularly known as the Ruptured Duck.

It was a small gold-colored emblem that looked like an eagle with its wings spread as if flapping in preparation for flight. The image of the eagle was partially outlined by a small circular band. While we were going through the process of being separated from the Service, we were issued and sewed the emblem on our dress uniform. This gold-colored insignia let the world know that we were new homeward bound civilians.

We also were issued small Ruptured Duck lapel pins, which we could proudly wear on our civilian jackets or coats. This insignia of pride let people know that we were honorably discharged veterans. I still have mine.

COLLEGE

Wearing new civilian slacks and a sports coat with my Ruptured Duck pin in the lapel, I went to San Jose State College to apply for admission. After presenting the registrar's office with my Honorable Discharge paper and my GED diploma, I was accepted on a first probation trial basis as a freshman for the fall quarter of 1946. They were giving me a chance to see if I had the ability and determination to earn a college degree. This was not uncommon. There were quite a few other veterans with GED's who were also being given this special privilege to further their education.

Most of the younger incoming students had completed four years of high school. Many of the former military personnel entering or re-entering college under the GI Bill were two to ten years older than the average freshman. Quite a few of them were former officers that had completed one to two years of college before they went into the service.

As veterans, we were trying to make the transition from the military to civilian life and to catch up for the lost years. The war, military service and the resulting GI Bill gave many of us a second chance. This was especially true for the older students (twenty-three to twenty-nine years old). The opportunity and the privilege of going to college were not taken lightly.

The incoming college students in the fall of 1946 were a unique group. The freshman class of 1946 had a span in age of ten or more years—not counting the differences in our life experiences. Almost all of us were born between 1918 and 1928; we had all lived through the Great Depression of the 1930's. An atmosphere of more mature direction and purpose prevailed. We were the residues of war, attempting to put our young, disrupted lives back to a semblance of normalcy. Sitting in the same classrooms with eighteen-year-olds that had just graduated from

Pat, Agnes, and Jim Reding with Boots the dog. Notice the ruptured duck on the right chest of his uniform.

four years of high school were combat veterans, some of them were amputees or disfigured. To blend together such dramatically diverse groups was a real challenge for the administrators, faculty and students. Somehow the blending did occur.

Personally, with my limited academic background, it was a reach for me try to compete with the older, more experienced or better educated students. It was not easy; I had a lot of catching up to do. I don't regret going into the Navy, but I certainly wouldn't want to go through those experiences again, nor would I wish them upon anyone else.

CAMPAIGN MEDALS AND RIBBONS

The campaign medals and ribbons earned by the crew of the USS *Fergus* (APA 82) were:

American Theater of Operations Medal and Ribbon
Asiatic-Pacific Theater of Operations Medal and Ribbon
Philippine Liberation Ribbon
Philippine Victory Ribbon
World War II Victory Medal and Ribbon
Occupation of Japan Medal and Ribbon

BIBLIOGRAPHY

Browne, Courtney. *Tojo, The Last Banzai*. Holt, Rinehart, Winston, 1967.

Costello, John. *The Pacific War*. New York: William Morrow, 1981

Dodson, Kenneth. *Away All Boats*. Annapolis, Maryland: U.S. Naval Institute Press, 1954.

Fahey, James C. *Ships and Aircraft of the United States Fleet*. Victory Edition. New York: Ships and Aircraft, 1945.

Farragut Idaho State Park, Visitor Center Information Service Pamphlet.

Frank, Benis M. *Okinawa, Men and Battle*. Talisman Parrish Book, 1978.

Leckie, Robert. *Okinawa, The Last Battle of WW II*. New York: Penguin Books, 1995.

Lorelli, John A. *To Foreign Shores*. Annapolis, Maryland: U.S. Naval Institute Press, 1995.

Moore, Arthur R., *A Careless Word . . . A Needless Sinking*. American Merchant Marine, Museum, 1983.

Reding, James, personal diary and ship's photographs, 1944–1946.

Island Fighting. Time Incorporated, Time-Life Books, 1978.

USS *Fergus*, APA 82, Ship's Log, February 1945 to June 1946.

USS *Fergus*, APA 82, crew remembrances from ship's reunions, 1990s.

Blue Jacket's Manual. Annapolis, Maryland: U.S. Naval Institute Press, 1943.

U.S. Navy Cook Book, United States Government Printing Office, 1944.

Walsh, Douglas. *The USA in WW 2—The Pacific Theater*. New York: Gallery Books, 1982.

INDEX

SHIPS, MILITARY AND CIVILIAN ORGANIZATIONS

Army

United States Marine Corps,

United States Merchant Ships

United States Navy Ships and Squadrons

Other